Seasons of Life

Extraordinary Life of an Ordinary Soldier

Seasons of Life

Extraordinary Life of an Ordinary Soldier

Maj Gen Purshotam Vig
AVSM, VSM (Retd.)

Vitasta

Vitasta Publishing Pvt. Ltd.
New Delhi

Published by
Renu Kaul Verma for
Vitasta Publishing Pvt. Ltd.
2/15, Ansari Road, Daryaganj,
New Delhi - 110 002

ISBN 978-81-89766-85-6

Cover Design and Layout by Vitasta Publishing Pvt. Ltd.
Printed by Vits Press, New Delhi

To My Family

Contents

Section-II

My Thoughts

Section-III

Life As I See It

Preface

Torn between the urge to go deep into the mystery of life and reality of living, I wandered into the labyrinth of mythology, religion, philosophy of life, history and literature. The mystery kept deepening till I chose to introspect and trace my life in bits as these surfaced in my thoughts but not chronologically. The fog started lifting. The mystery started demystifying. I did not have to go far. Episodes from my past and my observations about life had a tale to tell. It took me some time to decide if I had a story to tell about myself, when there were far higher achievers in my field. But my observations and reflections about life interwoven with my experiences synergized the tale. I felt there was a message. A message of inspiration. Inspiration to perform and retain the balance to be close to the nature and life; to be involved, yet be detached; to savour every moment that life had to offer.

Encouraged by this rationale, I ventured to proceed further to share my story and thoughts. The message is for one and all, transcending the barriers of age, sex and borders. This book is autobiographical in concept but with a difference. It is an anthology of my experiences interwoven with essays on vital facets of life, my reflections and narratives of my adventures and sports activities, which have been a vital part of my life. To that extent, each chapter is comprehensive in itself. The reader, therefore, has the flexibility to read the book from any chapter.

Little had I imagined the transformation from a humble beginning to a successful career spanning over nearly four decades in the elite Indian Army, clawing my way up inch by inch by shear hard work and toil, that too in the technical stream which has a steep pyramid. Profession remained my primary focus, but furtherance was never in the plan. I was content with what I got and never set my sights high. There are no guarantees for furtherance in the Army. However, the selection norms, though tough, are absolutely fair. One also has to be lucky. I have enjoyed my share of luck. My professional contributions were formally recognized, leading not only to my rise to a two star general, but also in conferring of distinguished services awards, twice by the President of India and once by the chief of Army staff.

On the extracurricular front, I had a serious handicap of my background. Being physically weak and with little or no exposure to sports, I had to cover a lot of ground. Thanks to my edge in intellectual field, I could focus more on this aspect. With time and phenomenal effort, I went on to become not only physically tough but even excelled in many sports and adventure activities including representing the country in one. All this was nothing short of a miracle. Interestingly, I am continuing to pursue these with vigour till date though deep into my retirement. I have come to realize that such a miracle could not have happened overnight. It has been a long journey. A journey of sustained effort and perseverance. After all, life is like a long distance run. Short sprints and flashes here and there are of little relevance. I owe this to my having remained natural in thought, transparent in behaviour and positive in attitude.

I love nature and respect the sensitivities of life. Observing emotive facets of life inspires me to remain firm on the terra firma. Reading has been my habit since my early years. It has only flourished ever since. This has given me an insight into the wisdom of great scholars and thinking minds. Relating to all this has rejuvenated me with self confidence, inner strength and mental resilience. In all humility, I dare say that it is a rare combination of attributes and attainments. Hard it may seem, but I have enjoyed doing all these, at my own pace, managing my time sans any stress and strain. Providence has continued to shower its blessings as a bonus in keeping me youthful not only at heart but also in looks. This is the essence of my life, and this is what I intend to share with my readers.

I was not in the habit of maintaining a diary, or even keeping notes about various benchmarks or about random thoughts on my views about life. I never felt any need for these, as I hardly like to live in the past. Somehow these remained embedded deep down in my subconscious mind. It did take me some time to decide to pen these down, but when I did, digging into the hazy memory was a wonderful experience. A pleasant journey back in time, down the memory lane. The haziness was lifting, surprisingly with relative ease. At the end of the tunnel, I could clearly recollect my experiences, as if photographically etched in my mind. How did this happen? It is still a mystery. Possibly because these are straight from the heart. All transparent, with nothing to hide.

Purshotam Vig
Maj Gen (Retd)

Introduction

Picking up threads from the book, varied thoughts unfold. There is an incisive view of life starting from a serene and blissful environment to the shattering impact of the Pak-sponsored attack on the valley of Jammu and Kashmir in 1947 and the recommencement of normal life thereafter in the early years of the author's life. The events unfold with his growth, neatly interweaving his varied and rare achievements. Be these in the thoughts going on in his mind before his first jump to qualify as a paratrooper, or to hoist the national burgee atop his sail boat when representing his country in an international yachting regatta.

The author describes, in a simple manner, the nuances of the command of troops and that too of a technical unit, where an ordinary soldier could be an expert in his technical field. His focus on improvement at the grassroot level paid rich dividends and was the hallmark of his command. Thrown in are many rare and inspirational achievements. In the senior ranks, he describes the professional intricacies, his incisive analyses and the manner in which he and his teams were able to handle the challenges, be these in a strike corps to keep the equipment of the formation in the highest state of operational preparedness, or in handling the personnel and administration affairs of Eastern Command operating from Fort William. Yet another interesting resume unfolds the challenges that the logistics throw up. We get the first hand view of the author who headed the logistics and administration of Western Command for a long period of nearly three years including during the crucial period of Operation Vijay, code name for the Kargil operations. Heading the Electronics and Mechanical Engineers in the Northern Command, he focussed on those who contribute in a big way to the war effort by keeping the tanks rolling, the guns firing, and the communication networks ticking, in a live operational environment, yet remaining in the background. These were the technical personnel, whom he viewed as the unsung heroes. With time and effort, the paradigm shift in the attitude to recognize their effort was visible. The same personnel went on to achieve many rare technical feats, enhancing the operational preparedness of formations of Northern Command.

The book leads us to an interesting journey thereafter, dealing with myriad views on matters of life. Starting with the live topic of retirement, the preparation for it and how to deal with the issues that we all have to confront one day or the other. The author threads us through the sensitivities of various facets of life like love, loneliness, memories, reading, aspirations and many more. There is a message in each of the thoughts including in the traumatic experiences of pain the author experienced and overcame. He shares his rich experiences in each of these thoughts applying the incisive analyses to his own life. It is a learning experience to share his thoughts and achievements in various fields of sports and adventure, be these in a car rally, in squash or golf for that matter. Overall the book is an expression of the journey of his life and his observations about life. There is so much to pick up from this journey.

Acknowledgements

This book is not really a book. It is a journey. A journey through decades of moments lived bit by bit. It is a journey about my thoughts and observations. Writing about myself has been the most arduous endeavour for me. I can't boast of an elite background or of extraordinary achievements. Yet, I realized that it was a rare mix of many facets of life. The dilemma between self-aggrandizement and self-denial of the due only compounded the issue. Writing in the first person about myself was like making a public confession. How much to tell? How much would be acceptable and readable? I was not sure. I was apprehensive, rather reticent. But reliving many events of life continued to trigger a shiver up my spine. I felt I had a story to tell, a story which could inspire many inquisitive minds across the barriers of age. This book is not my show alone. It is the sum total of direct or indirect efforts and influences of many. I gratefully acknowledge their contribution.

I owe my existence and my values to my parents, both now in their heavenly abode. I have imbibed inner strength and sensitivity towards life from their selfless love and care. My sisters, both elder to me, have ably continued to depute in their place guiding and holding my hand.

I owe my gratitude to my family; my wife, two wonderful children and their spouses who have encouraged me to flourish, respecting my decisions about my life, irrespective of the possible impact on them. I am thankful to them and to my sister for having vetted my writings, and for making efforts to reach some of their friends for a second opinion and for giving me an honest feedback and encouragement to proceed with this project. I am particularly grateful to my son who lives in New York, for his constructive advice and my daughter for her unstinted effort in making this project see the light of the day. I am also thankful to my granddaughter for the secretarial help which she was to provide, but graciously delegated back to me because she is only five.

I am thankful to my teachers who triggered the fire in my belly; fire to seek knowledge. I am extremely thankful to the National Defence Academy, my alma mater, for transforming a raw adolescent like me into a vibrant young officer of the elite Indian Army.

I have deep gratitude for the Indian Army and within that my own technical organization, namely, Electronics and Mechanical Engineers, for nurturing me and giving me ample opportunity for learning and growth. I am indebted to my senior colleagues for their patience and being a motive force for me. I am particularly indebted to my brother officers and the men who were members of my team for their whole-hearted support and for giving shape to my thoughts and sometimes even dreams. But for their unstinted efforts, this story would not be there to tell.

I am grateful to my publisher and their editorial staff for their painstaking efforts in giving shape to this work.

I am grateful to the famous thinker, J Krishnamuthy, for his works on matters of life. These have left an indelible imprint on my mind.

I have been deeply impressed by Thomas Hardy. His sensitivity to observe the simplicity of life and nature and the powerful expression of the same has been captivating. I am also grateful to the Noble laureate, Orhan Pamuk, whose writings in his famous book, *Other Colours*, have been a source of inspiration to me.

I am thankful to the Internet, the web media, and to Google. But for them, I would have been totally stranded. I am particularly grateful to the Wikipedia in their elaborate network and research on so many topics. I have often fallen back to them for clarification of my thoughts on many issues. Picking from Chetan Bhagat, the author of *Five Point Someone*, I too am thankful to Bill Gates for Microsoft Office, without which this project would have remained muddled in my poor handwriting.

Finally, I wish to state that, while I have browsed various sites, read a lot to help frame my thoughts, the concept is mine. The views expressed about various issues during my service in the Army are my personal views, as perceived by me. If I have faltered or failed to give due credit for any issue covered in this book, it was purely unintentional and inadvertent, which if brought to my notice, I shall unhesitatingly rectify.

About the Author

Maj Gen Purshotam Vig, AVSM, VSM (Retd) was born in 1944 in picturesque township of Baramulla of the state of Jammu and Kashmir. Followed by turbulent initial years, he surprised himself by opting for and making it to the elite National Defence Academy. He was commissioned in the then Corps of Electrical and Mechanical Engineers of Indian Army in 1964. In the course of his eventful career spanning nearly four decades, he acquired high-end qualifications both in the technical and executive channels. He held many key and prestigious staff and instructional appointments both in his own discipline and on the general staff. A rare honour for a technical stream officer. Keeping the focus on profession, he would still find time to pursue his interests in reading and in the outdoors.

A qualified engineer, the author holds masters in three varying disciplines: Electronics (communications) from the Army, Business Administration and Defence Studies. Besides, he is an alumnus of Defence Services Staff College, Wellington, Higher Command Course, College of Combat, now Army War College and a fellow of many prestigious technical institutions.

He was conferred with the Presidential awards for distinguished services, namely, Vishisht Seva Medal following command of the battalion in 1985, and Ati Vishisht Seva Medal for his contributions in the operationally active scenario in the Northern Command as a Major General. In addition, he was awarded the Commendation Card by the Chief of the Army Staff for his contributions in a strike formation as a Brigadier in 1994.

On the extracurricular front, he is an adventurist, loves nature and outdoor life. He qualified as a paratrooper and was a part of the elite parachute formation. The author has been and still is a keen squash player, an ardent golfer and a proficient yachtsman. He has fair achievements in these sports to his credit including having represented the country in yachting.

He has an inquisitive mind and is a keen observer of life. His urge to go deeper into the philosophy of life has triggered his passion to diversify his reading in many directions giving him an insight into various facets of life. Setting a personal example, he has led his officers and men from the front. His style of leadership has been simple, forthright and transparent; without any discrimination. Creative by nature, he encouraged innovation, infused professionalism and a spirit of confidence in one and all, thereby creating an environment for growth. He is a rare combination of an intellectual mind, an ardent adventurist and above all is full of compassion. His achievements in varied fields are a rare mix. He was considered to be a source of inspiration and a role model by many. He hung his uniform in 2002 and lives with his wife in Panchkula, India. He is actively continuing with his literary pursuits besides regular squash and golf.

Section-I
Life As It Unfolds

1

My Early Years

Be not afraid of greatness: Some are born great, some achieve greatness and some have greatness thrust upon them....
- William Shakespeare in Twelfth Night

I saw the light of the day in Baramulla, a remote township of the princely state of Jammu and Kashmir. The year was 1944. We were a family of four. I had two elder siblings, both sisters. Mother, very motherly. Father, a competent, and an upright forest officer. I learnt he was handpicked by the Maharaja for this forest-rich area, as forests were the main source of revenue of the state.

Digging deep into my subconscious and hazy memory, I recall Baramulla as a picturesque town with lush green ambience. Backdrop of the imposing snow-clad Shamsabari Range and the famous Nastachun and Razdan passes was simply breathtaking. Baramulla had large green meadows where wild flowers bloomed at will. Daffodils and hydrangeas were the most common. Chinar and walnut trees dotted the entire area. The air was pure, days bright, and the nights starry. The town was split in the middle by the Jhelum River, the lifeline of the Valley. I loved the *shikara* and houseboat rides. I recall that the people were very friendly and affectionate, irrespective of their religion. Everyone seemed to know everyone else. I would love to run up the meandering path through the meadow near our house. Ours was a typical Kashmiri house with traditional architecture, best suited for the cold climate in the Valley. There were many attics and corners in the house, some of which were my favourite hiding places. I enjoyed every moment of this state of bliss.

However, all this came to an abrupt end in 1947. In the wake of Independence, efforts were on to consolidate the Union of India by merging the princely states. Pakistan subverted the process of dialogue and launched a preemptive attack on multiple thrust lines. The Uri-Baramulla-Srinagar axis was raided through its sponsored irregulars, the Kabailis. For want of adequate resistance from the state forces, the raiders progressed well. They managed to sneak up to the periphery of Baramulla town much faster than anticipated. There was panic and chaos all over. We were fortunate to be hastily evacuated to Srinagar airfield in a cargo truck, packed like sardines, and wearing multiple layers of clothes, as no baggage was permitted. I moved like a robot and felt excited about the travel ahead. I had absolutely no understanding of the gravity of the situation and what must be going on in the minds of the elders in losing all their earthly possessions. Nor could I understand the impact that this chain of events was to hold in store to shape our destiny. Unlike the most convenient response, I don't recall my parents ever discussing the finances, or the shortage of the same, and any anguish on what all they had lost.

We were lucky to be airlifted to a safer haven in Jammu. Thereafter, we moved on to Timarpur, a refugee camp in Delhi. Ironically, it was my first flight; an Indian Air Force plane, a Dakota. The child in me saw this as an eventful flight, but for my family, it was a flight for survival. My next flight was going to be 19 years later, when I would make my first jump to earn the wings as a paratrooper of the Indian Army.

We were not the only ones undergoing the trauma of such a displacement from our hearth and home; there were many more. I was to learn later that my wife to be, who was then not even a toddler, was also stuck along with her parents in the far interior area of Gilgit, annexed surreptitiously, and later retained in Pak Occupied Kashmir. They were less lucky, for they could manage to escape only on ponies, traversing tedious routes astride the higher reaches of the mountains.

Our stay in Delhi was not very long. We waited eagerly for things to stabilize back home and to move back. Life in Delhi was totally different. Small house, blazing heat, unbearable humidity, and high pressure dust storms in abundance. Life there was a far cry from the caresses of cool air and pristine beauty of the Valley. We yearned for the climate and the ambience that we had left behind. Notwithstanding the privations, the inmates of the camp quickly developed a bond with each other. They would often congregate and recapitulate their past and discuss about their future plans. They would celebrate and suffer together. I recall that out of all the joint celebrations, Holi was celebrated with great gusto. I somehow abhorred these celebrations, and would prefer to hide under the bed. Our family made many lasting relationships in this refugee camp. In spite of the restricted facilities, we developed a liking for this environment. Finally, we moved back to Jammu by middle of the next year.

Our initial stay in Jammu was with my maternal grandparents. We were anxious to pick up the threads from where we had left and bring our life back to normal. My mother took care of the family and my father resumed his official duty. It was in Jammu where my formal schooling began. However, I was averse to the school and was ever reluctant. I would often make flimsy excuses to avoid going to the school. Finally, my grandfather took charge. One day, he locked me up in the store. Thereafter, I posed no problem. I not only became a regular but also started enjoying going to the school. This was particularly so because I had a great company in my cousin brother. We were in the same class and had a healthy competition, inspired by the incentives offered by our grandfather. He had affectionately nicknamed us Gulu and Mulu; I was the latter. He would give us a feast of *rasgullas* to our hearts' content if we both stood first and second in the class. Whatever be the trigger, this actually started happening. My cousin was usually ahead of me, but this was only till school level. Thereafter, I beat him with a big margin.

During our summer vacations, we all would visit our father who was invariably posted to the interiors of the state where the forests were rich. Some of these places were Batote and Banihal. The ambience of these places was out of the ordinary. Pine and deodar trees gave us a refreshing reprieve. Their fragrance was intoxicating. The wind would whistle through this coniferous family of trees. We would enjoy long hikes, swimming in the rivulets, and relishing apples, peaches and apricots even before these were fully ripe. In the absence of any other form of entertaining activity, we would retire early for the night.

Whilst we enjoyed every bit of our holidays, the massive homework for the vacations was irksome. This kept us busy for the better part of the day. I enjoyed going out on tours deep into the forests along with my father. We would stay in a tented camp in a hamlet, meeting the locals, mostly Gujjars, and learning about their way of life. They were simple and contented people and were happy in their solitude. They enjoyed the world of their own. They were solely dependent on the forest produce and their cattle for survival. Salt, sugar and kerosene oil were their primary necessities from the 'other' world. These would invariably have to be humped up to their log huts. Ironically, their life hasn't changed much even five decades later except for some areas where Pak-sponsored terrorists have disrupted their peace, finding these areas to be safe havens.

My physical growth was far from adequate. In fact, I grew up as a weak child. However, my mental faculties made up for the physical. Mathematics was my favourite subject. I remember having helped my elder sister, who otherwise was a brilliant student, with mathematics, although she was a class ahead of me. I seldom had to buy new books for the higher class as the complete set would be handed down by her, as good as new only till they reached my hands. Within a short period, there would be notes scrawled and underlines all over. In the school, we had a section called Golden Section where the top 30 students would be grouped together. I had the privilege to be a part of it. The teaching was focussed and the level pitched high. Our English teacher was a role model for us. He was the trigger for the fire in our bellies. He created an environment where one could cross the barriers unquestioned, and be innovative and creative. This infused in us a spirit to strive for excellence. It, therefore, did not come as a surprise to us when many of the top positions in the university in the final school leaving exam were garnered by our class. I was one of them.

At home, my growth was dominated by the feminine majority. I wasn't effeminate, but I wasn't strong and manly either. Outdoor sports were neither easily accessible nor was there any specific urge for the same. However, I had a restless mind and my mental faculties afforded me ample opportunity and time to learn and excel in wider activities. I was very good in indoor games like chess, carom, and cards. I learnt chess from my grandfather. The challenge to beat him was my ultimate goal and it remained so even in my adult life. I don't remember making any materialistic demands from my parents; never felt the necessity for anything specific.

We three siblings had a room to share, which also housed a make-shift study table at the ground level. We would squat on three sides and study. The fourth side was earmarked for stacking the books. My corner was always messy. Being a restless mind, I would invariably break the seriousness of the atmosphere during the common study period, particularly when my sisters were concentrating. None of us ever felt the necessity of tuition. We were fortunate to still do well in our own fields. My eldest sister went on to earn two master's degrees, in Economics and English; the next one became a doctor with a doctorate in her subject. I was among the top few in the university, both in school-leaving and undergraduate levels. This set the stage for me to be offered admission to a number of top engineering colleges. One of these was at Chandigarh, which I joined for a few days, till I went for an interview by the Services Selection Board for admission to the National Defence Academy (NDA) for a commission in the Indian Army. This decision was to change the course of my life. One was to reflect, though much later, whether at that time it was a rational decision for me or otherwise. I, being a physical weakling, though academically bright, would have a lot to catch up in this profession, if selected. Answers to all these were to unfold only with the passage of time. But what emerged loud and clear was that with our focussed minds and the grace of God, restricted or lack of facilities did not come in the way of all three of us to achieve fair heights.

It was fateful. To my utter surprise, I did get through the interview for the NDA. The only hitch was that I had to undergo tonsillectomy and put on a lot of weight in the next three months. I did both, one surgically and the other by eating a dozen of bananas on the re-medical day. This cleared the decks for my joining the NDA. All along, I wondered what exactly they were looking for leaving out tough and smart guys and picking me up. I was to learn later that their focus was on leadership qualities, character values, moldability, and potential rather than on physical attributes.

A completely different kind of life awaited me at the NDA. The new ground I was to tread was totally unfamiliar to me. I had no idea of the military life, nor was I mentally and physically prepared for it. I had to face this all by myself. One could not even discuss such issues with anyone. But I matured very fast. The journey through NDA and through my long career in the Army is a history in itself. By strange coincidence and by the grace of God, it turned out to be a success story with considerable achievements, though at a huge cost and effort to me. But I have no regrets. The decision to join NDA and thereafter to join the particular branch I chose were all mine. The latter decision had a vital bearing on my growth in the Army. Nonetheless, I graphically remember every moment of this journey. I have enjoyed every bit of life then and am continuing to do so now. I am sure I wouldn't have been any different even if it had not turned out this way. But when it came to my son, in all fairness I put the cards clearly on the table with all the pros and cons.

As luck would have it, I passed out from the NDA and later from the Indian Military Academy among the top few in my batch. In the Army, I rose to be a highly decorated two star general in a technical support cadre, which has a very steep pyramid. I was privileged to wear the maroon beret, and became a sportsman of sorts. I donned the national colours in yachting, played squash at a high level, and became a decent golfer; all this for that weakling, who had not even heard the names of yachting, squash and golf before joining the NDA. I think it was nothing but a miracle.

Surprisingly, against all advice and odds, I continue to be very active, including in squash. Maybe it is God's way of chastising me for having been so pretentious. Incidentally, I did visit Baramulla later, and was appalled to see that it had lost its beauty and had been virtually turned into a fortress, thanks to terrorism and its sponsors in our neighbourhood. From a nondescript town in the backyard, its name has since been splashed on the international map for no better reasons but terrorist activities. I pray and hope that good sense prevails and life returns to normal.

2

My First Jump

Brave are not necessarily those who are not scared.
But those who do not show it.

Setting: Higher reaches of ski slopes overlooking famous mountain resort of Gulmarg. Year: 1966, fresh from 1965 operations. Scene: The penultimate day of the winter warfare course that I had volunteered for. Schedule: Preparation for the grand finale of the course, that is, for the slalom and downhill competition. Atmosphere: Full of excitement. One of the toughest courses, having successfully trained more than a hundred officers and other ranks of the Indian Army to be reasonably confident ski troopers, was coming to an end. The directing staff were satisfied and smiling. As if all this was not enough, I received my marching orders to join the elite parachute brigade on culmination of this training. What a timing! It appeared too stage-managed to be true to step from one adventure to another. Little did I realize the deep impact this move was to have on my life and career. Although I had volunteered to be a paratrooper soon after my commission into the Army, I had little hope, for I was from the technical stream which had very few vacancies for officers. The technical support component is a mere fraction of the combat component. I was thrilled by the news. In fact, I was dazed and slipped into a reverie, only to be shaken out by a loud uproar of the felicitations.

Gulmarg, at that time, was at its harshest best. The snow was delayed, but was in plenty. The temperature was subzero, but the slopes were conducive for good skiing. There was vast expanse of white blanket, and the trees were drooping under the load of snow. The scene was picturesque and beautiful, but not for us. We were not tourists; we had a business to attend to. We obviously missed what the tourists pay a fortune for mere short stays there. There were no ski lifts in those days, so one had to trek up the slope using ski skins on the fresh powdery snow. It was tedious and enduring. The skis and other gears were also not state of the art. All this only added to the challenge. Those who were physically fit could take it in their stride. I did too. It was a lot of fun. Once on top of the slope, coming down was only a matter of seconds. I would invariably carry my Voigtländer, a SLR (Single Lens Reflex) camera with me. Loaded with memories, we dispersed. I was ready to move for my new assignment.

At the earliest opportunity, I reported to my unit in the parachute brigade. Paratroopers the world over are considered to be men apart. They all wear maroon berets and a wing. They are tougher than the normal soldiers of respective armies because the selection criterion has higher physical standards of battle efficiency on ground, besides ability to reach deep into the enemy territory without the aircraft having to land. This demands a higher level of mental toughness for the Para-dropped force to be on its own till the link-up takes place.

The demands of being a paratrooper started sinking in. The posting was notional. One was on probation to be tested for physical and mental toughness to meet the criterion for a paratrooper. Only then would one be permitted to wear the maroon beret. The wings would be earned only after successful training and minimum number of day and night jumps. In short, the men apart did not accept anyone below their level. No wonder they pitch and maintain their standards high.

I qualified in the physical and mental tests with relative ease. The toughest test was a 40-mile long night march with full load and against time. The catch was to lead the entire batch of men who also were being tested. I beamed with pride when the commander presented the maroon beret to me. However, the main event was yet to come. Soon I was informed about the basic parachute course. This was conducted by the para jumping instructors. They were super fit and meticulous trainers. Their instructions were precise and have remained graphically etched in my memory till date. These had to be followed strictly, for any mistake could cost life. Each one of them had several hundred jumps to his credit.

After a brief introduction to the entire sequence, we were put through the ground training to learn the techniques of all the stages; from the jump to landing and stepping off the harness. The distinct stages were: jumping out of the aircraft, free-fall descent, deployment of the parachute, controlled descent, nearing the ground level, landing, and finally, deflating the canopy. The landing techniques were vital to avoid injury. I learnt that the body had to be kept taut, knees firm and bent in crouching position, chin tucked in, right hand firm on the rip cord handle of the reserve parachute, and toes stretched up. All this was to ensure that the touchdown was a two-point landing, flat on both the feet. We were taught how to diffuse the impact of landing by rolling in the direction of the wind. Thereafter, it was vital to deflate the canopy quickly by turning it around leeward, failing which the inflated canopy could drag the paratrooper like a toy, causing grievous injuries. Was I now ready to jump? Not from the aircraft yet, as we had to go through rigorous ground training.

We practised simulated jumps from aircraft mock-ups at varying heights on ground and finally a harness-aided jump from a high tower. This gave us a fair idea of the feeling one was to get when standing on the edge of the aircraft mid-air with the door open. Next part of our training was to understand about the parachute, its packing and characteristics of the aircraft. All these were very important. After all, jumping off the aircraft is a risky business.

The parachute is a huge canopy, approximately 30 feet in diameter, sufficient to create adequate drag to reduce the rate of descent for a safe landing. Made of synthetic fabric, it had a number of triangular segments stitched together and assembled by lines to give it the shape. The segmentation is an in-built safety feature to arrest shearing of the canopy, if at all. The lines were attached to the harness for the paratrooper. Parachutes are designed in different shapes of canopies. For paratroopers, a round shape was preferred. We had the main parachute packed in a bag that was worn on the back, and a reserve parachute worn on the chest. The main parachute would be deployed by static line hooked on to the aircraft at one end and to the top end of the parachute by a snap ring at the other. As the paratrooper jumped out, the static line would pull out the chute from the bag. Once fully stretched, the snap ring would snap and the canopy would be filled by air. All this was to happen in four seconds. While in free fall, the paratrooper had to count and look up. If the chute had deployed, fine; if not so, then he was to deploy the reserve chute by pulling the rip cord handle. It was a backup, but not in full. Since the size of the reserve parachute was smaller, the landing would be hard. Our parachutes were not steerable, but they did give limited manoeuvrability. Static line jumps ensured positive deployment of the parachute and minimum spread of the paratroopers. We also learnt how to pack and inspect our own parachutes.

The aircraft had two side doors, both used for simultaneous jumping of two sticks at a time. It also had a rear opening which was suitable for dropping heavy cargo by sliding it out on a platform hooked to a cluster of parachutes. The drop was invariably carried out against the wind, commencing just short of the dropping zone and finishing well before the end of the zone. This would facilitate deployment of the parachute ensuring entire landing on the dropping zone, which in operations ought to be secured in advance. Simultaneous exit from both the doors, if not timed to the second, could cause a mid-air collision and entanglement of the paratroopers. Learning about all the vulnerabilities, I began to wonder how safe it was to jump. We had learnt about various types of malfunctions possible, but drew solace from the established casualty rates, which were miniscule.

In the heat of the moment, one really did not care. It was time to relax and collect my thoughts for the first jump.

The much-awaited moment finally arrived. It was rather early in the morning. The weather was a bit hazy. The sun was struggling to break through the crust of thick fog that had enveloped the sky. Soon the far end of the horizon turned crimson red, heralding the arrival of the sun that emerged majestically and grew into a huge fireball. It was too close, perhaps the closest I had ever seen. We took our seats in the order of the jump. I was to lead the jump from the port exit. We slid and double-checked the hooking of the static line to the cable in the aircraft. The atmosphere was serene, rather quiet. Everyone was brooding or reflecting on what was in store. We were not anxious, but perhaps curious. Was it fear of the unknown? May be. Our stomachs were churning, but we showed nothing. The façade was intact; emotions were not visible. Only the cold stare and the wait. We had taken off from the air base; the dropping zone was only a few minutes away. There was no air traffic. The aircraft took a long circuit to get into the wind and aligned itself to the dropping zone. Once close to the drop point, a red light flashed inside the aircraft, and we all lined up. The exit doors were opened. I stood on the edge of the door, looking right in front, into the oblivion. Soon the green light came on, followed by a yell, "green on, go". And I jumped out.

Suddenly, I was sucked down with great speed, the wind whizzing past with whistling noise. I was hurtling down like a stone. I felt as if I was sitting on the nose of a rocket in a nose dive with its tail on fire. As per the instructions, I had to count for four seconds and then look up. I didn't know what was happening, but whatever it was, it was happening too fast. Those four seconds were like a lifetime. Suddenly, everything stopped. All was quiet; everything came to a standstill. I looked up only to see a wide canopy above my head. The parachute had deployed. It had arrested the free fall. I was floating, and got a feeling of moving upwards like in a balloon. I looked around to see many paratroopers floating nearby, most of them looking lost like me but in a state of bliss. We were quite close to each other yet not too close to get entangled. Wind was moderate and so the drift was nominal.

It was an amazing site. In the far distance, the Taj Mahal looked marvelous. Shrouded in mist and bathed in a soft red glow of the morning sun. Down below, the ground looked distant and very smooth. The ground teams looked like pygmies. I spotted an ambulance in attendance and was reassured. The olive green parachute canopy fully filled, looked imposing and majestic with the sun peeping through the aperture. It was our ride. I was exhilarated and felt like a bird, gliding at leisure. I wanted to shout and sing. But the presence of the troops restrained me from any emotional display of joy. This was the most enjoyable part of the jump. Alas, all this was to last for too short a time. The entire jump lasted less than a minute. As we came down further, I experienced a strange phenomenon. The ground was moving upwards and that too at a very fast pace. It was the relative movement. The smoothness of the ground as seen from above had been replaced with roughness; its furrows, undulating folds strewn with lumps of earth and stones were now visible. Everything was approaching us very fast. Reflexively, I wanted to tuck my legs further up to avoid the impact. But that would have been disastrous, leading to a three point landing, dangerous for the spine. Soon, I was distracted by the warnings blaring from the loudspeaker from the ground control. The near ground level actions had to commence now. I tightened my body, got into the proper posture when approximately 20 feet above the ground. I landed safely, mercifully not with a thud, and rolled with all the agility I could muster. I got up quickly, deflated the canopy by turning it through half a circle and eased out of the harness. I had completed my first jump successfully! The entire episode looked too simple and too short. Once on the safe hardness of the ground, I reflected if that was all. I was to realize later that it was not as simple as it appeared. Every jump was a unique event and had to be error free. It was thorough preparation and meticulous training which made the jump look simple.

My second jump was again a great experience. But I was not as lost as in the first one, particularly in the first four seconds which matter the most. I had my wits in my control, and could count: one thousand, two thousand, three thousand, four thousand, and look up. This time I observed much more and focussed on the operational part of the jump. Para jump is only a means of reaching an area. This time I took stock of the time I had at my disposal during the cruising mode. It was approximately 20–25 seconds. I was getting ideas. More confident, I toyed with the idea of carrying my camera on the quiet. I practised taking out the camera, shooting, and zipping it back, all in 12 seconds flat. I could do it. And I did, in the next jump. This was one of the most thrilling snaps of my photography career.

The last few jumps had a degree of difficulty added. These were to be night jumps, simulating what one would undertake during operations. These differ from day jumps as one relied on the instruments primarily. It was pitch dark. The sky was clear, stars distant, and the moon in the last quarter. There was dim light visible on the ground underneath. Possibly, it was the ground control. It was very quiet, and I felt lonely. Oblivious of the surroundings, I had to focus and keep time to watch for 'nearing the ground level' stage. Even in a pitch dark night, there is always some ambience light. With effort, one could sense the ground when nearing it; rest of the actions were the same. I landed safely, and was one more step closer to earn the wings.

I learnt later that one of the soldiers had made a grave mistake while stepping out. He stayed too close to the aircraft, and consequently, his chute was caught in the slip stream. It was partially torn. He was in panic but somehow managed to deploy the reserve parachute. His landing was rather hard. Since he was hurt, he could not deflate the canopy and was dragged, which aggravated his injuries. He had to be evacuated. He survived but had multiple fractures. All this was taken in stride and did not deter the rest of the force from becoming too protective.

On completion of all the jumps, I became a full-fledged paratrooper. I had earned the wings. They were pinned on me in a mini investiture ceremony by the commanding officer. I proudly wore it throughout my long career. I had now become a part of the men apart. But this was not end of the challenge. It was only the beginning. I had been put on a higher pedestal. The degree of challenges had increased; the bar had been set higher. One could not just live on one's laurels; one had to continue to excel. I always felt inspired, energetic and confident amongst this group of high performers. Courage of conviction is the hallmark of a good paratrooper. There was no tension; the attitude positive, environment creative and conducive for growth. I learnt all this in this great organization, the parachute brigade, and imbibed these traits reflexively. In retrospect, I feel it was not merely the jumps, but being a part of the maroon berets that triggered a paradigm shift and transformed my life.

3

The National Burgee

God, allow my mind to soar like a bird
And sail like a boat, full and by.

The year was 1970. Backed by a rich experience of six years, including the 1965 operations and tenure in the famed parachute brigade, my posting to the prestigious NDA as an instructor came as a pleasant surprise. I learnt that such a posting at the given stage of my career was like a feather in the cap. In the normal course, it would be a stepping stone for many more. Time only was to tell if this would be true in my case also. In any case, for me, it was like homecoming, back to the alma mater where I had been groomed not very long back.

The NDA had a plethora of facilities and offered a variety of activities. To me, this opportunity was God sent. I wanted to savour all that I could not pursue as a cadet. In addition to squash, which I was fairly proficient in already, I chose to pursue yachting with vigour. This was an obvious decision for me. I was enamoured by the very sight of sailboats. They looked fabulous in the vast expanse of water. A sailboat skimming over the surface of water with its sails fully filled was a majestic sight. Manoeuvring a boat in strong winds and that too against the wind direction always intrigued me. And I wanted to face this intrigue headlong. I yearned to be in a boat.

As regards our home front, on our relocation to NDA, we settled down fast. We were just married, and did not have too much baggage. We were allotted a spacious house with a sprawling lawn. We had good neighbours. Scenic hills surrounded the campus. I had a well-set routine, with little or no professional pressures. One couldn't have asked for more. My wife, fresh to the military life, adapted to the new environs with amazing grace. With plenty of activities to pursue, she too started liking this place. Life was like an extended honeymoon. In short, NDA offered an ideal opportunity for growth.

On the professional front, I was to be in charge of a very well-equipped cadets' workshop to impart training in nearly all aspects of general engineering practices. Fresh from the engineering course, I thought this would be a cakewalk. But not until I found some cadets to be amazingly talented and highly inquisitive to learn advanced techniques. For this, a hobby club was established where such cadets were offered ample opportunity and guidance to undertake complicated projects. These projects would later be prominently displayed. Smart and athletic cadets working intently in small groups, on as many as 50–60 machines of a wide variety, all under one roof and all at the same time was an imposing sight. No wonder the cadets' workshop was always a must stop for the visiting dignitaries, including the likes of heads of various countries, or of their armed forces. Once I got my foothold in my profession, it was time to pursue yachting. The Naval Training Team, which was responsible for running the Sailing Club, appreciated my enthusiasm and welcomed me with open arms. The sailing activity was undertaken in the adjoining Khadakwasla Lake.

Khadakwasla Lake is a massive freshwater lake. It had been created artificially by a dam trapping the rainwater and a perennial rivulet. Both the lake and the dam derive their names from the adjoining village Khadakwasla. The reservoir is nearly 6 miles long and 1.5 miles across at its widest end. It is the main source of freshwater supply for the city of Pune. The lake is overlooked by a thickly-forested hill range which extends along the NDA. It offers a breathtaking view from the Academy's guest house for visiting dignitaries, located atop the overlooking hill. This point also doubles for the vantage point for panoramic viewing of the yatchting regattas. The sight of the fleet of sailboats racing away at full speed and their elegant manoeuvres is worth every moment of viewing. From the far side, reflection of the hills in the water and their hues and profiles changing along the stretch is captivating. There were strong wind shifts closer to the hills. With experience, I learnt the impact of these wind shifts on yachting in these waters. Winds were generally strong there; they built up during the day, and peaked in the afternoons. In summer, the winds would become gusty. I learnt to gauge the speed of the winds by the presence of turbulent waves and their size, appearing to be white. In sailing parlance, these are called white horses.

Winds would die down after the rains, and the lake would look flat like a mirror.

I was given a brief orientation to the basics of sailing and an introduction to the naval jargon and its universal terminology like fore, aft, bow, stern, beam, line, halyard, sheet, port, starboard, types of knots, safety measures, and so on. I was also given a cursory idea of the fundamentals of the 'rules of the road at sea' and basic rules of sailboat racing in both individual and team events. With time I realized that an in-depth knowledge of the rights of the way in open waters and the rules of racing was vital. Cardinal rules in sailing were the right of way of a leeward boat over windward boat; a boat on the starboard tack over that on a port tack; overtaking boat to stay clear; and the more manoeuvrable boats giving way to the lesser ones. Yet, the safety factor would be overriding. Besides these, there were many dos and don'ts in sailing which I had to learn and follow.

The Sailing Club had a variety of sailing dinghies. The Enterprise class was a popular choice. Enterprise is an international class sailboat used for both racing and cruising. It is made of glass reinforced plastic with built-in buoyancy tanks. It is a two-man boat, approximately 13 feet long and 5 feet wide, with a total sail area of both the main and jib sails being approximately 115 sq ft. In those days, spinnakers were not deployed on this boat for racing. Given its material and design, Enterprise was a highly unstable boat. The crew had to be vigilant all along. I was to start my sailing career on this class. Being a novice, I was allowed a Tindal, that is, a trained seaman, as my crew. He was my friend, philosopher and guide till I gained sufficient confidence.

Initial outings were aimed to get the feel of the boat and its controls, which were not many—the tiller to change the direction, the sheets to trim the sails, the centreboard to control the friction under water, and a single crew to order about for everything. The mystery of windward movement of the boat became clear now. It was not merely the force of the wind but a combination of the aerodynamic force generated by the aerofoil design of the sails and the hydrodynamic force generated underwater by the forces acting on the centreboard. The jetty was located well inward, so there was adequate time to practice in mild wind before hitting the open waters. Thereafter, there would be no respite.

First of all, I realized that there were no brakes in the boat. My guide taught me that a sailboat never sank even if it capsized. He further taught me that a capsized boat could be righted fast with skill and agility, and set on sail without loss of much time. I also learnt how one could avoid a capsize. This was easier when sailing against wind. These lessons gave me tremendous confidence. Reassured of the safety, I introduced my wife to this sport as my crew in due course of time. I learnt the techniques to steer the boat; tacking, when going into the wind, and gybing, when the wind was behind. The crucial issue was to execute these manoeuvres with speed, so that the sails would fill up fast and the boat maintained its momentum in the new direction. This was followed by learning various techniques of sailing. These included beating into the wind, or sailing close-hauled, going on a reach, and sailing on a dead run.

In close-hauled sailing, I learnt the importance of trimming the sails and balancing the boat. I also learnt the art of keeping an eye for the flutter of the luff, the highest point of the main sail, to sail closest to the wind, sufficiently close to move fast, to avoid keeling over, and not too close to be pinching or to go into irons. In short, essence of going upwind was to keep the boat stable and balanced and sail close, yet maintain the momentum. To cater for the displacement from the target, I learnt the need to go up in a zigzag route as the boat could never go directly into the wind. Depending on the skill of the crew and a well-tuned boat, one could go anywhere from 35 to 45 degrees close to the wind. This area on either side of the direct wind direction was a 'no go' zone. In a race, the first leg is normally a beat. Therefore, mastering the technique of close-hauled sailing is vital to gain an early edge in a race. I realized that close-hauled sailing technique is the acid test of a good sailor. Knowledge of fine tuning of the boat for better pointing upwind adds to the edge.

Sailing on a reach was a pleasure. With the wind at right angles, or from aft on a broad reach, the speed of the boat would be the fastest. With time, I learnt and mastered the technique of planing the boat, that is, by reducing underwater friction and lifting the bow of the boat above water. The boat would then skim on the surface of the water. It would virtually be riding on its own waves. The contact area with water and the friction would reduce, generating additional speed for the boat. For planing a sailboat, one had to be on a broad reach, the mobile ballast, that is, the crew shifted towards the stern and the centreboard pulled out. It was a difficult manoeuvre, but once mastered, the boat could fly past even the windward to their utter dismay. I loved to plane the boat, and with time, became quite proficient at it.

Sailing on the run should be the easiest and would hardly need any skills. This is what I had thought, till my boat went nearly over during the gybe and the beam shifted wildly. The most difficult event in a dead run is the gybe. The boat has to be kept in balance, the centreboard pulled out just in time, and the sails fully opened to trap maximum wind. Once all this is done, one can relax a bit. But one has to watch for the gusts and the wind shifts all the time. I was finding sailing very interesting and was ready to learn the finer points of racing.

First, one had to learn the technique of a good start. Once the warning guns were fired, the sailing rules were in force. Any infringement would imply a harsh penalty. Essence of a good start was to be clear of other boats, yet endeavour to be the most windward boat, and timely crossing the start line precisely on the start gun with the sails full and by. This would set up a flurry of activities in the start zone, with the entire fleet milling around in a limited area and jostling for an ideal start. I found the start to be the toughest part of a race. The course for a race would normally be triangular, mostly of two rounds. It gave ample opportunity to a good sailor to catch up in the second beat, if one did not get a good start. During the race, one had to apply all the skills learnt and the local knowledge of the wind shifts. One had to strictly follow rules for right of the way, yield when due to others and claim when due to you. Rounding a buoy, which usually marked each leg of the course, needed finesse. We had to be close enough to be the inner boat in time, yet not too close to miss the buoy due to wind shift. If too cautious, a smart sailor with a better pointing boat could sneak through while rounding. In short, there never was a dull moment throughout the race. We were under constant pressure from the winds and our fellow competitors. In team racing, the team tactics would further compound the problem. Although boats would be lesser, three for each team, but the tactics would be well planned and executed like a military operation. Notwithstanding all the observations, I found sailboat racing to be extremely absorbing and a true test of one's ability and agility.

I was a fast learner. My athletic build and sharp reflexes facilitated my becoming a good strong breeze sailor. In fact, I detested low breeze sailing. I developed a rapport with the boat and the controls like a rider with his horse. A soft pull on the tiller, mild trimming of the sails, tacking, and gibing with reflexes, all this was becoming a second nature to me. Baptized by fire of toil and sweat, and enthused by the passion for yachting, I graduated within an amazingly short span of time to be an important member of the NDA team. I was now confident to introduce my wife to this sport. She readily agreed and picked up the nuances fast. We both participated in a number of local races and even won some. Ironically, it was much later that I realized she was a non-swimmer. I really appreciated the confidence that she had reposed in me. I had the privilege to gain rich experience in a number of regattas and to contribute substantially to the team.

It was one of our summer breaks. The cadets had gone home. A number of well-known sailors of the country had come to the NDA. I learnt that they were to form a team for an international regatta to be held a few days hence. For such events, sailors with established credentials were called for the trials. In short, the participation was by invitation. Since the participants trickled in, there were a plenty of pre-trial practice races. The committee graciously agreed to my participating in their races. Fortunately for me and not so much for many of the established sailors, the wind conditions were strong. Huge sized white horses were a common feature. Being a local, and with an aptitude for strong breeze sailing, I outperformed a number of aspirants. Now the committee focussed on me. The crunch issue came when a few of the participants lost out due to gear failure, or injuries in the abnormal wind conditions. The number of sailors available for the trials dwindled and was becoming marginal. Running short of options and time, the committee included me as one of the contenders. To be catapulted to sail along the legends was the most exhilarating moment of my life. As luck would have it, the winds were at their gustiest. And I was a beneficiary of the nature's wrath. I did extremely well and wasn't surprised to be included in the national team, but with a rider that I was to crew for a senior member. Things were happening too fast for the fledgling sailing career of mine. I was counting my blessings.

Coincidentally, at the helm of my boat was another sailor from the NDA. So the NDA had the privilege to field one boat out of the three for India. As we were rigging our boat for the first race of the regatta, the officiating commandant, a naval officer, came by to compliment and encourage us. An accomplished sportsman himself and with a sharp eye, he looked up to the top of the mast and whistled, "Wow, the National Burgee! What a rare honour indeed," he said. A burgee is a pendant or a triangular flag flown atop the mast of a racing yacht to identify its team. In the heat of the moment and anxiously preparing for the race, we did not realize the importance of the tricolour pendant, which we ourselves had hoisted. The home team performed with credit and won accolades. The event was successfully over. Everyone shook hands and the guests departed.

We were back to our routine. I had all but forgotten about the event, until one day I received a parcel containing a complimentary letter from the Yachting Association of India and a sky blue blazer cloth, with 'INDIA' embroidered on the blazer pocket. Also embroidered were the name of the event and the five interlinked circles denoting the five continents, an emblem of the Olympics. I was thrilled with this surprise. It now dawned on me that I had been formally recognized by the national body to have represented India, that too selected amongst veteran and admired sailors, some of whom had devoted their lifetime to the sport. I felt guilty for having received the national level recognition with such a short sailing experience. It all happened very fast, but it was not my fault. I was perhaps the best bet at that point of time under those conditions.

I now became the toast of NDA, fellow officers and cadets alike. The cadets were already enamoured by my maroon beret of a paratrooper and my expertise in squash. To my surprise, I found quite a few top level cadets, including two gold medalists, opting for the technical stream of the Indian Army that I was a part of. I was specifically introduced to the visiting dignitaries as a national sailor. All this started sinking in well, till I was jolted when a similar introduction to the visiting Army Commander boomeranged. In a social gathering, the General jokingly pointed out to my wife, "Now that your husband has achieved this feat, he will ask for a posting to a good sailing station." This gave me the message that the Army did not require gladiators; they needed officers to lead men and to be with them. I kept this in mind throughout my service. Nonetheless, I clarified that I already stood posted to a field area and had not represented. So there was to be no more sailing for a long time.

During my tenure in the NDA, we were blessed with our son. In his brilliant career, he pursued squash and golf in his student life in India and later in the USA. I was also pleasantly surprised to learn that he had voluntarily taken lessons and had qualified to be a helmsman. On my next visit to the USA, he took me out sailing in the bay of New York City many times. It was an exhilarating experience, much beyond my imagination. I wonder if it was continuation of a legacy by design or by intuition.

4

An Oasis in the Wilderness

There is a treasure of happiness hidden even in the wilderness. You only have to look for it.

The year was 1982. I was a young Commanding Officer of the Electronics and Mechanical Engineers battalion of a formation. Our peace location was in a border township in the distant east in North Bengal, astride the national highway towards Assam. Though a family station, the local facilities were next to nothing. A broad gauge passed through the area, but the township was too nondescript to find even a mention in the railway map. The nearest railhead was three hours away. In short, the place was well-tucked in the interior, fairly inaccessible, and devoid of any urban facilities. The military station boasted of total seclusion and solitude. On the flip side, the location enjoyed reasonable immunity from external influences, giving rise to ample opportunity to cultivate a culture of its own. The essentials were provided for; the attitude professional, but positive and relaxed. The environment was conducive for growth. Warmth towards each other and mutual dependence was visible everywhere. Willingness for mass participation, contentment and happiness were writ large on everyone's face. All these factored to unify the garrison into a well-knit extended family.

Although the infrastructure of the station had been planned, but the execution was only half-way through. It housed lavish residential accommodation, large spaces for sports and training, a nine-hole golf course, a mini market, and an officers' institute. In short, given the limitations, the military station was like an oasis in the desert of this wilderness. It was our Shangri-La.

The entire belt was humid and rich in rainfall. The climate was conducive and the soil fertile. The region was flush with a large and rare variety of flora and fauna. Even more than two decades later, we are still carrying some of these rare varieties of the plants. The area was ideal for growth of tea. It has been aptly named the Dooars, that is, the gateway to the hills. It ushered in an ambience of vast stretches of lush green tea estates dotting the entire area. Some famous names like Nagrakata, Lankapara, Banarhat, and Birpara tea estates are still fresh in my mind. Each tea estate had a culture of its own. The people working on the estates work hard, but they enjoy even harder.

This part of North Bengal is enriched by the icy-cold and crystal clear water of rivers such as Teesta, Jaldhaka and Torsa. In addition, many streams and rivulets crisscrossed the area. On a clear day, the imposing Kanchenjunga peak offered mystical spectacles from different viewpoints. It hazily depicted the different moods of Buddha—lying, reclining, or meditating. The countryside was breathtakingly beautiful. One could picnic anywhere throughout the year. We often explored such spots. Thick forests and foliage, and abundance of water set an ideal breeding ground for the wildlife. The Jaldapara Wildlife Sanctuary, which was situated nearby, exposed one to joyful elephant rides, and breathtaking views of pure and untouched beauty of the big cats, a variety of deer, blue bulls and many more. In short, nature was at its best here, and we were fortunate to relish every moment of this rich abundance.

On the professional front, we got ample time and opportunity to train the troops unhindered. Some of our sister formations were deployed in the high altitude areas. They operated in snow-clad areas with attendant adverse effects on the equipment and personnel due to harsh working conditions. They had glamour attached to everything they did, including in failures. All their actions or inactions were recognized. These formations garnered all sympathies and priorities. We were like the poor cousins. We had to do something big to match. This was our challenge.

We shortlisted our core competencies and focussed on the key area of achieving excellence at the grassroot level. Training and competitions were imaginatively interwoven by our team, setting the fire in the bellies of one and all. Once the innovative mind was tickled, confidence became the hallmark of this outfit. Nothing could stop us from excelling. We strived to remove the word 'impossible' from our dictionary. Our teams started tasting success, and got further motivated. Working quietly and systematically, the state of operational fitness of the weapons and equipment of the formation was brought to an astounding level of nearly one hundred percent. This was sustained virtually from within our own resources. This was a rare feat and could not be kept under the wraps. Life was blissful thereafter.

Once the basics were in place, the tenure of my command was a cakewalk. There was no tension. The atmosphere was quite relaxed. My style of command was simple—forthright and straightforward; transparent, sans any discrimination; fatherly yet friendly. Recognition for excellence without any reservations and encouragement for the lesser performers. The aim was not to do down a failure, but to reinforce the strengths. Results mattered the most. Inter-personal relationship between us was warm and genuine. The level of motivation was infectious. The higher headquarters recognized this and were fully supportive. News of some unique or innovative achievement by our team would frequently pour in. Accolades would often follow, sometimes even from unknown quarters, congratulating us for our positive attitude, or the help rendered by our teams. The unit excelled both in its peace and operational roles. The confidence reposed from higher echelons was clearly visible. A number of additional and sensitive assignments were entrusted to us. We undertook all these in our stride. We worked hard but also found time to pursue extracurricular activities. My golf flourished further. I won virtually every tournament in the vicinity, including the annual event of the tea gardens.

On the social front in the garrison, our battalion families had a great bonding. They stuck together through thick and thin. Every major competition would end with a social event, and this would happen often. The children loved it. Picnics would be organized in the vicinity of our station at the drop of a hat. We explored virtually the entire countryside and relished every moment of it. All these gatherings had a tremendous positive impact on the growth of character and values in our children. They learnt the value of relationships early on in their lives. They learnt that there was no shortcut to success. They learnt that hard work and focussed preparation was the key. This done, any challenge looked simple thereafter, as was the case with the larger unit they belonged to.

In the course of time, I familiarized myself with the entire area. This included virtually entire Sikkim and North Bengal. Famous landmarks were the hill stations of Kalimpong, Gangtok and Darjeeling. High altitude areas of Sikkim included the famous Nathu La and Jelep La passes, besides the North Sikkim areas of Chungthang and the northern plateau bordering Tibet. These passes are at heights of more than 14,000 feet above the sea level along the Indo-Tibetan border, overlooking the Chumbi valley of Tibet. The entire ridgeline and these passes remain snowbound throughout the year. One has to acclimatize properly, failing which one would become vulnerable to hypoxia. Even for short exposures, one has to have strong lungs. With time, I learnt that I did have these. Thick fog would often set in and visibility would be reduced to a few metres. If not careful, one could drive off into the deep valley down below. Though a national highway connects Gangtok and Kalimpong to Siliguri, the road was narrow and prone to landslides. River Teesta, flowing alongside most of the distance, made driving more dangerous. Coronation Bridge on River Teesta at Sevok connects West Bengal to Assam. The bridge was built on a deep gorge and was an engineering feat. Driving to North Sikkim was a challenge in itself. River Teesta flows virtually throughout the stretch deep down in a gorge. The area is accident prone, resulting in phenomenal loss of life. I had a reliable vehicle backed by my good driving skills and reflexes. Therefore, I preferred to drive over the entire area myself. I did face some complex situations of poor or no visibility in the higher reaches, but managed to make it in good time. A faint-hearted co-traveller sat on the edge of his seat throughout the journey. Little did I know that my driving prowess was being watched and was going to be put to test in the near future.

On my return to the parent station, I was informed that a Jonga Rally was being organized and I was to be a member of the team from our formation. The Jonga was a light vehicle in service in the Indian Army. I was reluctant to join the rally and protested. My plea was that I had no experience of a rally, and as head of the technical battalion, my performance might reflect on my unit or my formation. I had too much at stake. I was advised to consider this as yet another additional assignment and represent the formation, which I did. It is another story that I did well and won it hands down.

The time of my command tenure was flying by. Unlike in most cases where there is pressure and anxiety, I had a free run. I even felt guilty for enjoying my command without working for long hours unlike many of my colleagues. I believed in sustained performance with natural capability and strive to achieve quality results. After all, we are participating in a long race of life. Neither is it possible to sprint throughout, nor do the flashes in the pan make any difference. It has to be a sustained effort all along. In short, the essence is in improving the productivity.

Individually average but collectively super performers, my bunch of officers surprised me more than anybody else. No wonder they were instrumental in giving shape to my ideas and turned an ordinary technical unit into a vibrant all-round outfit. The grapevine said that the formation headquarters considered us as one of the best units in the formation. If true, it was a rare compliment for a technical support unit. We were cruising well.

All this lasted until one fine day a rude shock woke me up from my dream. I received my posting order. Like all good things, this too came to an end. They gave me the barest minimum tenure. Probably they had seen what they wanted to see. How I wanted it to last forever! It was my privilege to receive, soon after this tenure, the coveted award of Vishisht Seva Medal conferred by the President of India for distinguished services. I was obviously elated, but hardly considered myself worthy of this stupendous recognition. If at all, I felt it was a recognition of the spirited and selfless contribution of our entire team, whose fond memories I still cherish with nostalgia. I dedicated this award to our team.

In reflection, I wonder if this station was indeed in the wilderness. If it was, then the end results proved it wrong. It stood out loud and clear that it is the people and not the place that make or mar the environment. We can always make our life miserable even in the best of the stations and yet be happy in the wilderness. It is the attitude towards life and one another which is the key.

5

On Jonga Rally

Success comes to those who have grit to take risks,
Nerves to endure risks and wisdom to prepare for risks...

The year was 1982. I was posted as the commanding officer of the technical and maintenance battalion of a formation in a remote military station in the east. It was a nondescript border town in North Bengal. The scenic but sensitive state of Sikkim, bordering Tibet and Bhutan with attendant sensitivities, was within earshot. As a norm, we were encouraged to familiarize ourselves with the entire area. Adventurous by nature, I was fond of travelling and exploring. I was thrilled to have such a mandate to explore varied but amazing terrain and picturesque landscape. There were vast stretches of tea gardens, meandering mountain roads snaking their way through the valleys and the mountain sides overlooking deep gorges. Breathtaking views awaited us at every turn. Snow-clad peaks of the Himalayas and the famous passes astride the Tibetan border offered rare sights.

I was childishly looking forward to take off. Once settled in my main charter, I carried out a whirlwind tour of the entire area at the earliest given opportunity. Being a confident driver, I chose to drive myself to get the feel first hand. It is only then that I realized the nuances of the varied terrain and the constraints for large-scale movements at a short notice. I thought this trip to be professionally most enriching. I also felt that such an exposure should be extended down the line to all field officers. It was a strange coincidence that similar thought had also crossed the mind of our higher formation commander. In fact, he had already issued directions towards this.

On my return, I was amazed to learn that a Jonga Rally was being organized by our higher formation. Jonga was a variation of a jeep in service in our Army. Four Jongas with a crew of four each were to form the team of our formation and I was to head one of the Jongas. I offered that as head of technical setup, I should not take part as I had no experience of a rally, and, more importantly, my performance may get linked to the performance of my unit and even of the formation. But I was politely overruled. So there I was, fully involved to participate in a car rally. The catch was that I had a lot at stake.

Before departing for the rally, I had my vehicle inspected and thoroughly prepared to check for the efficiency of brakes, clutch plate, suspension system, tyres, air pressures, pressurized cooling system, fog lamps, and tuning of the engine. The Jonga had an inline six-cylinder engine of nearly 4000cc of displacement. It was a powerful engine and thus ideal for mountain driving. However, unlike modern vehicles of today, fuel injection system of this vehicle was sensitive. If not driven in appropriate gear and speed, the carburetor had a tendency to flood, thereby stalling the engine in low speeds. Continuous running in that state could lead to overheating of the engine. One vital preventive measure for this was to ensure a highly filtered fuel. We recommended chamois leather filtration for every filling. In the mountains, one had to be ruthless for this.

The teams congregated at Sukna, our base near Siliguri. We were briefed on the rules and regulations of the rally. Although adventure was the main aim, safe driving was the theme. Each Jonga was to have an officer, but anyone of the four members could drive. I chose to drive myself throughout. No additional gadgets and navigational aids, including radio communications, were permitted on board. GPS system, cell phones or hand-held long range radio sets were not on the scene in those days. In short, once the rally was on, the team was on its own with no communication with other members, or the base. Jonga was a fuel guzzler, so the only modification allowed was to fit an extra fuel tank. Notwithstanding this, sufficient refilling points were established en route.

The rally was organized to cover the main arteries of the higher formation over four days, covering a total distance of nearly 1,000 km. This included stretches in the plains, semi-mountainous, mountainous and high altitude areas over 14,000 feet above the mean sea level. The rally was to be controlled by timing the rallyists at the control points on each leg against the ideal time. Speeds were specified for various sections of the route. Besides the start and finish points, four or five control points were to be established each day. Location of these was not known to the rallyists. So the acid test for the rallyists was to drive in ideal time for each section of each leg throughout. This was going to be tough. The scoring system was simple. 10 penalty points for being too late and 20 points for being too early per minute at any control or finish point. There were other penalties too; for minor and major accidents, for stopping the vehicle en route, for mechanical failure, and finally, for infringement of the traffic rules as per the law of the land as applicable. By and large, these rules conformed to the international rules of motor car rallying, except that in the scoring system, there was no differentiation in penalty for being early or late, unlike in our case.

The route and the ideal speeds for various sections had been selected very imaginatively by the organizing committee. The first leg covered semi-mountainous terrain and the plains stretch of North Bengal. The route was Sukna – Kurseong – Darjeeling – Teesta Bazaar – Coronation Bridge – Dam Dim – New Mal – Chalsa – Mainaguri – Binnaguri – Banarhat – New Mal. A 280-km long stretch. The second leg was New Mal – Gorubathan – Labha – Pedong – Rhenock – Rangli – Padmachen – Kupup – Nathu La – Gangtok. A total distance of 260 km. This involved crossing over from North Bengal to Sikkim via the alternate route astride the Indo-Tibetan border. The stretch from Kupup to Nathu La was more than 14,000 feet above the mean sea level. The third leg was the least complicated. We were to move to North Sikkim and return to Gangtok. The route was Gangtok – Mangan – Chungthang – Lachung and back. A total of 250 km. Chungthang is situated at the confluence of two rivers which merge to form the famous Teesta River. Lachung is at a height of 9,000 feet. The last leg was the shortest. It was Gangtok – Rani Pul – Pakyong – Rhenock – Pedong – Kalimpong – Coronation

Bridge – Sevok – Siliguri – Sukna. A total of 170 km, from Sikkim back to North Bengal, joining the national highway NH 31 after Kalimpong.

Sketch of the Area

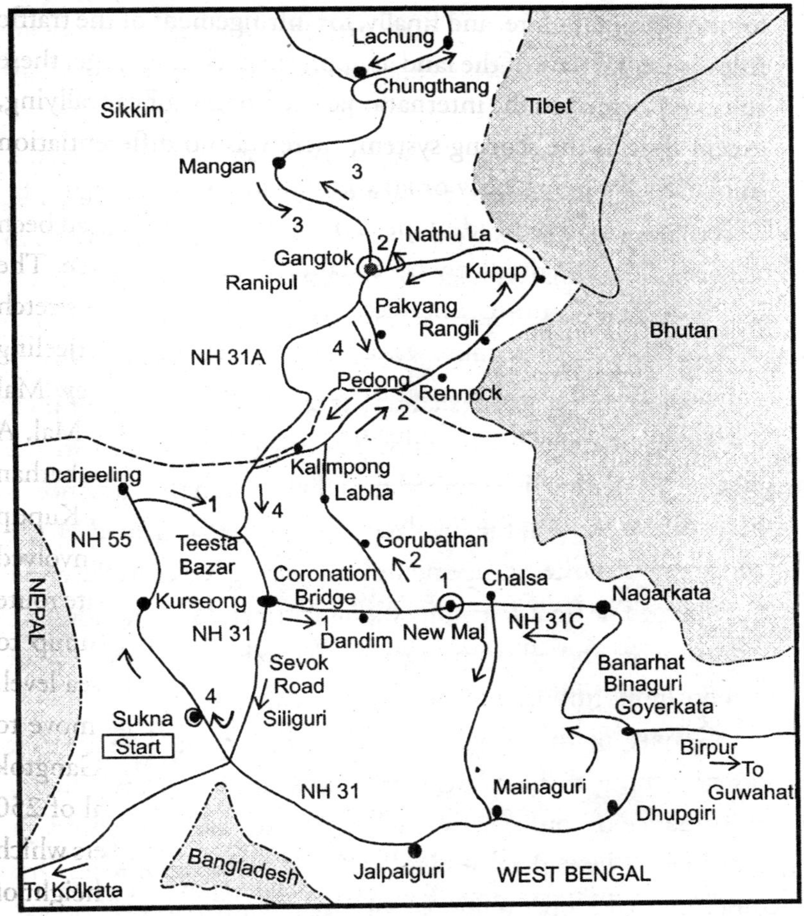

Note: 1, 2, 3 & 4 denote the respective leg of the rally

Not to scale

Planning of the entire event was carried out meticulously. It was executed with the finesse of a proper military operation. One was to learn all this as the events unfolded. The flagging off ceremony had been planned with great fanfare. The Army commander flew in to review the arrangements and to meet the participants. Radio communication had been established en route. A running commentary of the progress was broadcasted to update the formations and respective garrisons. Elaborate arrangements had been made by the formations to witness the rallying Jongas passing through their areas and to encourage their own teams. Similarly, flagging off for each leg was planned thoroughly. The Governor of Sikkim flagged off the rally on the final day from Gangtok. The Chief Minister of Sikkim also met the participants and wished us luck. He even announced special prizes for the winners. Entry of the rallying vehicles was stage-managed for a ceremonious finish in the stadium at Sukna in the order of their individual position in the rally. The biggest surprise was the standing ovation which awaited the rallyists from the audience in the stadium. Sensing the involvement and frenzy created by the rally, the level of the arrangements kept getting hyped as the event progressed. The final ceremony was just stupendous. In short, the arrangements and effort to organize this rally were indicative of the enormous importance this event had assumed.

Gravity of the situation started sinking in. I realized it was not going to be a mere drive around. An extraordinary performance on our part was warranted to befit this grandeur to display at least the semblance of a professional effort. One could not make any excuses later of lack of any past experience, of mechanical failure, or any reason beyond one's own control. After all, the champions prepare for four years for the Olympics taking every factor into account. They prepare, plan and peak on the final day. We were lucky. Our time frame was much shorter. The rally was starting the next day. This event had to be taken rather seriously. This set me thinking.

I huddled together with my team to plan our strategy. We analysed the entire event and discussed our response to possible situations threadbare. This was to be a zero-error drive over vast stretches of distance and time. For this, we had to be in ideal time at every control and finish point. With the locations of the control points being held back as a state secret, this rally was nothing short of a test of nerves for us as it required assessing these locations accurately. While we carried out an in-depth assessment of the likely locations of the control points, there was a method in madness. These control points could pop up anywhere, which they did in many cases. What emerged was that we had to be running in ideal time virtually throughout, and if not, we had to cut our losses by stemming the deviation to the least. In that case, one was to stretch the driving skills to the extreme. I had to do this many a time. I had to resort to driving at mad speeds of 70–80 km per hour in dangerous stretches to the amazement of my teammates. The sum total of these discussions was that each member had to be fully involved and double up for each other. They were supposed to be vigilant all along and assist me to remain focussed in my driving. Fundamental principles of hill driving were well-known and were extremely relevant in this case.

The Jonga had to be in top condition of mechanical fitness throughout. There was to be no complacency on this. My team ensured this. Driving skills had to be focussed to meet the challenges of each section, be it a continuous steep climb, or a gruelling downhill drive. Sudden accelerations and decelerations were to be restricted to avoid overflowing of the engine. Quick shifting of gears was the key to use the power of the engine to control the speed of the vehicle, rather than rely totally on the brakes. Double declutching technique was a must to shift into and out of the first gear, this gear not being synchromesh type. Each section had to be analysed in depth and ideal timings for each stretch tabulated. Equipped with a well-marked map, a calculator, a stop watch, a tabulated sheet and a host of calculations for alternate speeds in case of delays, we were ready and raring to go. While my teammates made the final checks of the vehicle, I took time off to relax and collect my thoughts for the first leg starting the next day.

The Army Commander personally flagged us off in an extremely impressive ceremony. We had drawn lots for the order of the flag off. Mine was 33, one of the last. Later I realized that this was also the designation of the formation. Once the chequered flag came down, I drove off with pride and elation. We had suddenly been catapulted into Himalayan Car Rallyists to the admiration of the clapping audience. They started believing that we were out of the ordinary. My heart was thumping; one had to live up to their expectations.

Once out of the stadium, one got focussed. The first section was vital; it was a steady climb throughout to Darjeeling, though steep at places. Ideal speed for this section was only 40 km per hour. It appeared to be low, but as the rally progressed, it actually turned out otherwise. I planned to maintain the ideal time in blocks of five minutes, but later reduced it to two minutes. To make up for the lost time due to external traffic, I had to drive at breakneck speeds many times. The next stretch was a steep downhill to Teesta Bazaar. This was a tough route that was rarely frequented. The road was narrow and had sharp turns. The downhill incline was steep and continuous in many stretches. Ideal speed for this section had been deliberately kept as low as 30 km per hour. That made the matters worse because the vehicle had a tendency to roll down and gain speed, that is, the wheels would drive the engine. In short, the phenomenon of reverse power flow would set in. To check this, one had to constantly bring down the speed of the vehicle. It was a catch 22 situation. Gravity would accelerate the speed. But the ideal speed was very low. To achieve this, one had to drive in a low gear constantly. This made the Jonga susceptible to overheating. One also had to curtail use of the brakes to short spurts. This stretch became the nemesis of many who relied on the brakes alone because the brake drums would heat up, making it impossible to apply the brakes. In fact, some of the participants had trouble even making it safely down. Our driving skills were stretched to the edge. Fortunately for my team, our analysis of suitable driving technique of using the power of the engine to control the speed paid off. As we hit Teesta Bazaar, we were on the plains stretch astride the NH 31, heading for Coronation Bridge overlooking Teesta River. I anticipated a control point anytime. Sure enough, our assessment was dead on. We logged in and continued.

Rest of the route of the first leg was easy. We maintained ideal speeds virtually throughout. Highlight of this stretch was when we were passing by our parent station, it was a treat to see our entire garrison lined up on the highway cheering us. They were somewhat disappointed to see us towards the end not knowing that the order of flagging off was by draw of lots for the first leg. We finished at New Mal. I was surprised that our officers had already reached there and had established a mobile field officers mess. By the time I entered, they went into frenzy, breaking the news that our Jonga was leading the pack with only 20 penalty points. We were late by one minute each at two control points and in ideal times at the rest. I was to learn later that many participants including other members of our formation team had picked up massive penalty due to the Darjeeling-Teesta Bazaar stretch. We could not afford to be complacent. Unmindful of the result so far, we got on with our preparations for the next day which needed special attention, as a large stretch was to be over high altitude area. Keeping the experience of the day in view, we reviewed our analysis for the second leg. Hereafter, we were to be flagged in the order of the ranking. That added yet another challenge for us the next day, navigation.

We had the privilege to lead the rally the next day. Fortunately for me, I had traversed over this stretch, so I was confident of the route. Most of the second leg was a climb. First section to Labha was a fairly steep climb of 4,000 feet. Thereafter, it was a short downhill stretch to Rhenock and a continuous steep climb to Kupup. From Kupup to Nathu La Pass, the entire stretch was 14,000 feet above the mean sea level. We were fortunate that the day was clear and sunny and visibility was good. The trailing Jongas did have to face some problem, as visibility often drops drastically in this area in the afternoons. I remember having had a bad experience on this stretch when heavy fog descended and visibility dropped virtually to nil. So far, everything was going as per our plan. The weather Gods too had played up. We were able to maintain the ideal speed. We were therefore not unduly concerned about the location of the control points. We crossed over from Kupup to Nathu La pass uneventfully, and thereafter, safely rolled down to the finish point slightly short of Gangtok. It was late in the evening when I learnt that we had not picked up any penalty points during the second leg. We had extended our lead slightly. During this leg, we passed through some exquisite and scenic stretches. The formidable Kanchenjunga peak could be seen far off in the distance from Kupup. It presented an imposing sight. Rare orchids and rhododendrons inundated the entire ridgeline. Pitifully, one could not take eyes off the middle of the road to absorb this lavish beauty of nature.

The third leg was along the single artery to North Sikkim. This was a tough route. The road, though two-way, was relatively narrow with many sharp turns. The alignment was astride the cutting off the mountainside on one side and River Teesta flowing ferociously deep down in the gorge on the other. Being the only artery, there was fair amount of traffic. Any mistake could be fatal. It became an ordeal to maintain the ideal speed of 35 km per hour. To top it all, the organizing committee totally surprised us by positioning a control point within the first 20 km. It beat our rationale. There was no change of terrain; the stretch was virtually flat with steady descent, and it was too close to the start point. Our analysis obviously had been subverted. Rest of the route, including the return drive to Gangtok, was uneventful for us. We did have a close call being too early nearing the finish point, but managed to crawl in to lose the spare time. Later, we learnt that we were still the leaders with only 40 penalty points. We were one minute too early at the surprise pop up, which added 20 penalty points to our account. The lead was still beatable. I also learnt that the local formation commander, who often commuted from Gangtok to Chungthang, was astonished to learn that we had actually averaged a speed of 35 km per hour both ways. He felt that we must have driven at insane speeds to make up for the lost time due to heavy traffic en route. I had done exactly the same. I was in a state of trance, stretching my driving skills and reflexes to the hilt. I was totally focussed, inspired, though unmindful, yet in full control. In reflection, I wonder if I could or would do that again.

Flag off for the final leg was the high point of this odyssey. Both the Governor and the Chief Minister of Sikkim graced the occasion. We continued to lead. At Rani Pul, we peeled off to the alternate route from national highway to Siliguri. The stretch was virtually downhill till Rhenock. Thereafter, it was a short climb to Pedong, along the ridgeline to Kalimpong and then a roll down to join the NH 31. Rest of the stretch was good, except the heavy city traffic one had to confront while crossing through Siliguri. For Sukna, we had to head towards Darjeeling for a few kilometres and then peel off to the west. This was the easiest stretch of all. The finish point was located a bit short of the Sukna base. Once we all were in, the final rankings were announced. I and my team had won the individual championship hands down with only 40 penalty points; beating the nearest rival by nearly 200 points. To add, our formation team also had won the team championship. All the tension and fatigue seemed to disappear. That was the end of the rally. But the ceremonious end was yet to be. We were to make a ramp show entry into the stadium with our Jonga in the lead.

As I turned into the stadium, I was astonished to see the sea of humanity in front of us. The entire gathering rose to give us a standing ovation. The crescendo lasted till all the vehicles were in. It was a rare honour. I was overwhelmed. It gave the impression of a victorious army returning home. I was being hailed as the victorious leader. Such recognition for mere driving around! Or risky driving, or for the adventurous spirit. I think it was a combination of all. Although most of us were novices at this game to start with, but we had matured fast to render a decent performance. We seemed to have earned genuine respect of the audience. We had been turned into heroes overnight. I became the toast of one and all.

Compliments flew in from all directions. The media lapped it up. My performance was considered professional. Our achievement set off a wave of frenzy back home in our parent formation. Never in the history of the formation had a competition generated so much of enthusiasm and involvement of so many. Total credit to the formation commander for his vision and to his staff to have stage-managed this entire event with the finesse of professionals. On my part, I dedicated this win to my teammates in my Jonga. It is to their credit that our vehicle did not have even a minor breakdown throughout this arduous rally. It was time to travel back to our parent station and to be with our families, where a warm reception awaited us. Yes, the prizes from the state of Sikkim finally did find their way to us, but not before surpassing ample bureaucratic hurdles.

In reflection, I felt that an event like this, though risky, was a masterstroke by the formation commander to integrate his command by mass involvement. For myself, I relished the moment, but soon shook off the hangover to get on with my job. I had learnt it early that one cannot live on past laurels. The Army did not want gladiators. That much for the Jonga rally, the first and the last one for me. Notwithstanding all this, the entire proceedings remained buried deep down in my subconscious mind. I maintained no diary, yet each and every moment of the rally remained etched graphically in my mind, and I did not have much problem in recalling the same more than two and a half decades later.

6

Living on a Reverse Slope

Every reverse slope has some sunshine, be it for a short while.
One has to learn to relish the moments one can...

After a long stint in a remote area in the eastern belt of North Bengal, I hoped for a posting to a decent station, a station with good schools. To my pleasant surprise, it turned out to be Shimla, queen of the hills. I was to be on the general staff in the Command Headquarters Western Command, a privilege for a technical stream officer. I couldn't have asked for more. We were thrilled and eagerly looked forward to be a part of this beautiful and historic place. Although relocation pangs can be unnerving, we chose to play it by the ear. We had ample preparatory time for the move. We hoped this would give us a balanced start. Therefore, we decided to move at the earliest. Lock, stock and barrel, with two dogs in tow.

In the excitement of the impending move, we forgot to factor in the efficiency of the railways in the east. Train travel to and from the east was considered to be an adventure. Sure enough, in our case too, it lived up to its reputation. To start with, we were stranded at New Jalpaiguri station, the rail head, for over six hours. But the farewell team had a better vision. They countered this innovatively and a field officers mess was quickly established on site. Soon the scene changed into a lively one at the station. Life in the Army had taught us to learn to relax and enjoy even in adverse situations. And so we did. Finally, the train arrived and we got going. But at night, the train screeched to a rude halt. Two bogies had caught fire. There was no other alternative but to unload our baggage, and wait on the tracks for the relief train.

However, the final leg of our journey from Kalka to Shimla on the narrow gauge train lifted the image of the Indian Railways sky high. Launched nearly a century back, the narrow gauge train must have been a technological marvel at that time. The train was luxurious and inviting. The staff was very polite and helpful. The track looked like a meandering pathway passing through numerous tunnels. The journey offered us scenic variations throughout. The train snaked through townships and villages within a handshake distance. It moved at a laid-back speed. The entire journey was very relaxing. As we moved past Solan, which was midway, the snow-clad hills of Shimla could be seen. After passing Kiarighat ridgeline, Shimla was visible in its full grandeur. It had an imposing skyline. Snow was resting on the trees and on the hill sides. A mix of white and green on the ground and blue in the sky presented a heavenly riot of nature's colours. The sun was bright and clear. Cool and refreshing breeze greeted us as we inched closer to Shimla. The entire scene was breathtaking. One could not help but admire the nature for this extravaganza. No wonder this was the locale for picturization of many beautiful and romantic songs of Bollywood movies. Our excitement heightened as we approached Shimla.

Finally, our train chugged into the Shimla railway station. A reception party was waiting for us. A tall burly officer rattled out some incomprehensible instructions. Before I could get my wits about, I was being whisked away to the office. I overheard that my family would be escorted to the Holiday Home, after stopping for lunch somewhere. After a brief preamble by my new immediate superior officer, I was handed over a heap of classified documents in a matter of minutes. The officer obviously wanted to be relieved of the burden as soon as possible so that he could rush to his unit immediately to earn a short report, failing which his promotion would be deferred. Little did he realize that progression of career in the Army is like a long distance race, where sudden sprints don't guarantee promotions. But at that point of time, I was trapped between a smart Alec and a weak boss, who acquiesced by being a silent spectator of the proceedings. I was reminded of Bhisham Pitamah of the *Mahabharata* fame, who chose not to intervene when norms of civilized behaviour were being flouted blatantly. The essence was that I was expected to join forthwith and that too voluntarily. I had to decide whether I wanted to confront or to accept this as a service hazard. I chose the latter.

At the end of the day, I reached the Holiday Home. My family was waiting for me eagerly. When I informed them about the situation, my wife and children kept quiet. We reviewed the situation. Our induction plan had been totally subverted. The preparatory time on which our relocation hinged had vanished completely. To add to our misery, the nature had been more than liberal with the snow that year. This made the logistics a hazard even for those already established in the station. For new entrants like us, it was going to be a nightmare! We had to think of plan B. Unfortunately, there was none. Then started the blame game. Definitely, it was the timing of the move. The date of arrival itself was weird. It was 29 February 1984. But who could predict all this? A rude surprise had caught us unaware. The attendant issues of the real beauty of Shimla slowly started sinking in. Incidentally, the Holiday Home itself was located in Jakhu, the highest point of Shimla. It seemed very close to the heaven. In fact, it couldn't have got closer. It is nearly one thousand feet higher than Shimla proper. It was extremely cold up there.

The hunt for good houses led us to an open-ended trail. The station had beautiful houses in sunny and accessible areas of Longwood, Bemloi, Jutogh Cantonment and so on. But none were vacant. To top it all, the Holiday Home, which was a kind of guest house, could not be retained beyond a few days. The noose was slowly tightening. Then came a ray of hope. A private cottage situated close to the Holiday Home was offered to us, that too on reasonable terms. It seemed too good to be true. We sensed that there had to be a catch. There sure was; it was located on the reverse slope of the ridgeline, tucked in fir trees, and a good distance away from the road. I suppose the owner was desperate too, as there were no takers, and so were we. We too fell short of options. Everything matched and we took the deal. Other concerns like schools for the children and so on were addressed subsequently. We quickly settled down in the new ambience. And a new life began.

The cottage, though small, was beautiful and merged well in the dark green thick forest. There was a trekking path skirting the cottage. We found solace in the fact that some cottages were still farther ahead and we were not the only ones to be stuck on a reverse slope. The cottage overlooked the road down below. But there was very little movement on this road. Tall fir trees engulfed the cottage. There were two small open patches on either side. When the sun was overhead, its rays would filter down these patches for a short while at different timings. Thanks to the engulfing trees, darkness would set in earlier than normal, till another fling of the setting sun allowed sun rays to sneak through at oblique angle and liven up the ambience. The entire cottage would be lit up afresh with amber reflections. To keep us company during the day, the langurs displayed their circus skills, while flying foxes took charge once it was dark. The nights were very quiet and peaceful, but very isolated too. Fortunately for us, security was not a hazard those days.

We innovatively stacked most of our baggage in the cottage. A set of nine equal-sized boxes, with plywood sheet, a makeshift backrest, and mattresses were converted into a comfortable double bed. Each one of us knew who slept on what. Since the market was distant, provisions had to be well-stocked. Our lifeline for logistics was my *sahayak*, and a very responsive camp officer, whose assistance I would seek only in case of emergencies. This much of backup was sufficient. In any case, I had my car parked at the road head. Domestic help was irregular due to the isolated location of our cottage. This added to the burden on my wife. She still holds this against our Shimla stay. Vehicles were allowed to ply only on cart road, which is the periphery road. Hence, it was a culture for everyone to walk. Shimla receives heavy rainfall and the rainy season is quite extended. Therefore, an umbrella was an inseparable part of our apparel.

On the professional front, my job primarily was to deal with staff duties. The charter was a long list. It involved coordination in functioning of our headquarters and our formations down the chain on various matters. Coordination was sensitive and time consuming. One had to be meticulous and have a hawk's eye for detail. Any mistake could prove disastrous, particularly when dealing with civil administration. It was a kind of thankless job as it was impossible to please everyone. Yet, the job came with certain powers, giving me some importance. But all this would last as long as the going was good. There was no scope for any error. Hence, I was on my toes all the time. Inter-personal relations bailed me out from many precarious situations. Out of my charter, what I enjoyed the most were the aspects pertaining to command and control, defining charter of duties, of new accretions and their sub-allotments to the formations, and movements of the formations and the units. Though there was never a dull moment, with time, we had our checks and monitoring system in place. Life was smooth thereafter. This job gave me a rich experience and was the precursor for my selection for higher command course, a professional course which normally is the gateway for growth and higher general staff appointments.

We settled down rather fast and set up a good routine. Our son, who was then a teenager, enjoyed trekking to the school, but our daughter's school was farther away. At the tender age of nine, she had to carry a rather heavy school bag. Generally, I would escort her to the ridge and then peel off. But the return trek was tough on her, and as a result, she would often fall sick. My office was the farthest, nearly half an hour's brisk walk down and 10 minutes extra for the climb back. At a good pace, I would be sweating profusely at either end, be it summer or winter. I was fit, but became fitter. One could wear mufti (an alternate dress other than the uniform) on most days, so good suits and combinations along with a stylish umbrella were only in keeping with the fashionable Shimla. This routine, though harsh, was in full motion. Slowly, as the time went by, it started looking easy. Mandatory walks and healthy climate generated a feeling of well being in us. We were always charged with energy. In spite of all the constraints, we started enjoying life.

With time, we extended our activities. Within minutes of my return from the office, my son and I would roll down to the Raj Bhawan for a game of squash. A quick change after the game and we all would stroll down to the famous Mall Road of Shimla. The heritage buildings restored to their grandeur and artfully lit presented a great spectacle. The view of the valley from the ridge on a starry night was breathtaking. The ridge also doubles up for the water storage for Shimla. In fact, it is sitting on it. The Mall Road would be full of jostling tourists. Honeymoon couples would be in a world of their own. On weekends, St Beed's girls would add to the colour. The shops, well-equipped with a wide variety and top selections at reasonable prices were always overcrowded. Eating joints were in plenty and were very popular. Famous ice cream corner, and *mithai* (Indian sweets) and *chaat* (savoury snacks made of fried dough) shops were ever-inviting. After a stroll across the mall up to the famous or infamous Scandal Point, we would often saunter into the historic Gaiety Theatre, which was also the Officers' Institute, and finally trek back leisurely after dinner. All this packed in a working day. One wondered how one got so much of energy and will to do it.

Weekends were eagerly awaited. We would have picnic breakfast in the open patch near our cottage to catch the sunshine overhead filtering through the fir trees. This would be followed by a game of golf in Naldehra or Annandale, both an hour away by car. Naldehra is a very scenic spot. It is a beautiful lush green meadow. It boasts of possibly the oldest nine-hole golf course in the country. The bowl in the middle had tee boxes positioned around it. The landing areas are very tight. It is a zero error course. If not landed properly, the ball could roll off anywhere. The drives from the tees and putting on the putting greens would be the only shots with normal stance. The rest would be uphill, downhill, or side hill. I recall the 18th hole. The green was perched uphill. The fairway was very steep. If one did not land on the green or slightly above it, the ball would roll right back to the tee. Annaldale golf course is relatively flat. It is the only big flat ground in Shimla. It also doubles up for a helipad, stadium, parade ground, and a training area. In the forenoons, there would be many interruptions due to chopper movements. The fairways of both the courses crisscrossed around the central bowl, so one had to be careful. During winters, when it was too cold to play golf, we substituted this with a drive down towards Solan, find a sunny and open patch, and enjoy a nice picnic lunch. In short, we were relishing every moment of our stay in Shimla.

The dogs, both Bhutanese Apsos, were a great company. Beauty, the mother, was true to her name and had the most beautiful pair of eyes. She was elegant, lady-like and mature. We respected her. On the other hand, Scissor, the brat, was exuberant, affectionate and innocent. He had to be tamed. The langurs were a nuisance during the day. Beauty would set to task and chase away the langurs with a purpose, but Scissor would follow her blindly, looking foolish. My wife experimented once. To dissuade the langurs, she leashed Scissor on the railing next to the entrance door. It was comic to see how the langurs got wise. One day, a langur sat staring at Scissor from close quarters. Once he was sure that Scissor was leashed, he slapped Scissor and vanished!

Time flew by. Before one realized, it was the rainy season. It would pour for a while, and then clear up. After the shower, the forest would look fresh. Sometimes fog would engulf the entire valley. With the cloud base above the valley, one felt as if you could step on the clouds or float. After the rain, a big rainbow would often appear in the valley, with one of its ends meeting the ground. As per an old adage, there would be a pot of gold at this meeting point. Soon the approach of winter was heralded by cold winds. The temperature plunged down to subzero. But by now, we were equipped for it, and hence ready to enjoy the winter escapades with *bukhari* and what all. We had our share of fun with the *bukhari*. Sudden change of wind direction would cause a back draft of exhaust from the chimney. It would smoke up the entire house. However, later it was fixed. The weather was so cold that sometimes water would freeze in the pipes. However, electricity seldom failed. Beauty is that the rest of the routine remained unchanged. Since the schools closed down in winter, and I too was granted a few leave of absence, we moved to the plains to meet our folks. By the time we returned, decision had been taken to move the entire headquarters to the plains. That marked the end of our Shimla stay which lasted one year but two winters for us. Still, we felt sad to leave such an ambience, and that too when my turn to move to a big bungalow was around the corner. Notwithstanding the pangs of relocation and settling down in a new station afresh, guess who was the happiest with this move?

We felt nostalgic on departing from such a heavenly environment, although there were start up problems and life was tough in general. But we took all this in our stride and converted this into an opportunity. Our family came closer. My son got interested in squash and golf. We learnt not only to value every moment but also to live it well. We savoured the nature's bounty and its ever-changing moods. We would have perhaps missed some of these, if things were available on a platter. What more, the children learnt to be resilient. All this could not have happened if the spirit of adventure had not been kept alive. Fortunately, I was physically fit, but the mental toughness of my family surprised me, thanks to the reverse slope. It indeed was a great experience.

7

Dancing Trees

Surely lawns, trees, the setting sun, the moonlight and the rain are present everywhere.

It is we who are in a rush and forget to stop and observe, missing so much in life.

The year was 1990. We had moved from New Delhi, the capital of India, where I held a sensitive appointment in the Military Secretary's Branch, Army Headquarters, planning the careers of officers of our Army. I was posted to the military station of Vadodara as Colonel General Staff of our technical training institution. Vadodara is a historic city in Gujarat. After a while, I was allotted an authorized accommodation which was an earmarked bungalow, a surviving legacy of the past. It had a sprawling lawn with tall and majestic trees lining the periphery. There were Eucalyptuses on one side and Ashokas and Cypresses on the other. We were very excited about the prospects of moving in this ambience. In fact, our children had already fallen in love with it. There were some initial hiccups in the allotment, but finally we moved into this dream house.

It was a huge bungalow with a large acreage and a host of servant quarters. In fact, it was a full-fledged colony by itself and thus had attendant management issues, including upkeep of the property, keeping the inmates gainfully employed, and to ensure harmony in the system. My wife handled all this aptly.

The professional front had a challenge of its own. My job involved planning, coordination and monitoring the conduct of technical training of specified disciplines for officers and soldiers responsible for repair and recovery of the equipment of our Army. The training was multi-tiered. It aimed at imparting expertise in a graduated manner in keeping with the experience in service and finally leading to become an expert in the field. In case of officers, it led to masters' level in engineering, whilst in case of soldiers, it would be diploma level. With my experience as an instructor and exposure on sensitive staff appointments, I settled down rather fast and soon was in a position to contribute to the system.

I love watching trees, particularly tall trees. They are imposing and elegant. They make you look up at them with respect. They make you feel humble. They have a hypnotic effect and transport you to a different world. Your mind feels refreshed and you are at total peace with yourself. Your imagination is free to soar and cross all barriers. You drift into a state of pure bliss.

At the end of the day, after a hard game of squash, I would often relax in the lawn. I'd usually lie down flat on the back and watch the tree tops sway. The evenings were usually windy and cool. The strong breeze would make the trees sway, as if they were dancing to the tune of a melody played distinctively for their ears. They would sway, sometimes wildly and at random, but after concentrating for a while, their movement would appear to be in rhythm. They became my buddies. It was a pleasure to spend time watching them. There were some trees that were far apart, but two particular trees were quite close; close enough to brush against each other in every sway. One was much taller than the other and they instantly appeared as a couple. These two trees appeared to be very fond of each other like lovers. My daughter had named them Sohni and Mahiwal after a famous legendary couple.

As the folklore goes, the intensity of love between Sohni and Mahiwal remained unabated even against stiff resistance and coercive efforts of their respective families and the society. They were forcibly separated. But Sohni would often brave strong currents of the fast-flowing River Indus and swim across at night with the help of a hard baked pitcher to meet her lover Mahiwal. However, on a fateful day, the pitcher was cunningly replaced by an unbaked earthen pot by her suspecting and jealous sister-in-law. Sohni drowned in the heavy current. Mahiwal too gave up his life trying to save her. The family relented, but it was too late. The lovers united in death and became immortal.

As the wind whistled, the trees swayed in rhythm. They would elegantly move apart and then lunge towards each other. The rays of the setting sun would try to sneak through their leaves. The swaying trees, whistling wind and the setting sun were an extraordinary spectacle. The ambience was heavenly. One could not but thank God and praise the nature for its rich abundance.

As night approached and moonlight brightened, these trees would appear to take myriad forms and shapes. Their movement and swaying was akin to a ballet dancer dancing with nimble feet. The swaying of 'Sohni and Mahiwal' was similar to human-like movement of lovers dancing with gay abandon. Their elegance was breathtaking. They would dance in harmony to the accompaniment of the orchestra being rendered by the whistling sounds of the wind and rustle of the leaves. While this couple would appear to be the central figures of the ballet, those who were further apart would sway and dance to the rhythm in unison approvingly. In parallel, a similar act would be enacted simultaneously by their shadows. I would lose sense of time and could be retrieved only by interludes of sharp reminders from my better half for the next event of the day. Notwithstanding this, I would try to prolong this and try to continue with my musings as long as I could. I felt like an active participant in this entire ambience. Dreaming.

On a starry night, these forms would not be so clear. However, to be able to relish the ambience, all I had to do was to close my eyes for a while and then open them slowly. As my eyes got used to the darkness, the figures would become clearer. Tall, thin waist lines of the trees would merge into the darkness. Only the tops would be visible against the star light. The movements would be mystic but real.

On a calm day, a totally different scene would be presented. The trees would look withdrawn, thoughtful, brooding, and almost devoid of life. They looked despondent, in some sort of agony. Agony of separation like Sohni and Mahiwal. Looking longingly at each other but helpless to reach out. Waiting.

Lovelorn; imploring the winds to blow. Invariably this would happen, as it would not remain calm for long. I suppose the nature has its own ways of testing the intensity of love. Finally, it would oblige.

In my state of such reveries, I would often have an unusual companion, Fluffy, our German Spitz. Unlike me, who was engrossed in this blissful ambience, Fluffy was always restless, electrified with energy and ever wanting to play. But he was always discreet, waiting for any signs from me, showering affections. He even deliberately played the fool by his tricks like chasing running water of the pipe, begging on twos, rolling all over, etc. Just to draw attention and please me. If ignored for a while, he would quietly curl up in my lap and innocently look askance, but never grudging. I would feel humbled by this selfless love and would bow imperceptibly with gratitude.

The rainy season had its own beauty. Sitting in the verandah, sipping tea, I would watch the couple in love and other trees standing nearby, relishing the shower in the open. Water would drip down from whatever path it could find through the leaves. But some droplets would continue to hang on to the edges of the leaves, resisting. Reflecting light in various directions. As the rain would stop, winds would do the chores of wiping the trees dry. They would then look sparkling clean and fresh.

Nature continued to display its resplendence with regularity. Only the model would change depending on the season, time of the day, type of night, rain or no rain, and intensity of the winds. One thing was in common always, and that was the actors. The backdrop also changed and so did outsiders like me. I soon realized that we were mere visitors. The trees were the real occupants; occupants forever, till someone had the audacity to tame them or be heartless to kill them. With time, I was to be separated from them as my next posting came too soon.

I was to move out as an instructor in the College of Combat, later renamed as Army War College. Though a feather in my cap, it was a totally different field. Although I had a stunted tenure in Vadodara, it was a great learning experience to be in a technical university environment. I did find time to pursue many activities. My golf flourished here. I was back in my old form, and won virtually every event. I also had the privilege to score my first hole in one, a rare feat, or luck I suppose. This luck was only going to stretch on, as I scored two more later in other stations. Thanks to my job and my sports activities, I was fortunate to rub shoulders with many young and energetic officers. Many of them would surprise me later by recounting our pleasant association. The city of Vadodara thrives in art and culture, and is a centre of higher learning. Like many of my predecessors in the station, we too followed the popular trend. Our daughter chose to stay back in a hostel to pursue her graduation and other educational programmes in the university.

We had to leave this great ambience with a heavy heart and bagful of happy memories and my intimate association with the dancing trees. As we left, I wondered whether such a display of nature was specific only to this place and house, or did this ambience initiate me to respect nature all the more. Surely, lawns, trees, setting sun, moonlight, and rain are present everywhere. It is we who are in a rush and forget to stop by and observe. Missing so much in life.

8

My Years in Fort William

God give me the courage, to speak the truth,
and strength to accept the outcome with humility...

Setting: intense operational environment. Organization: elite strike formation in the Western Theatre. Wherewithal: world-class tank fleet, state of the art artillery, air defense systems, communication equipment, heavy mobiles, and a plethora of specialist equipment of combat and logistics support systems. Terrain: semi-desert. Event: conduct of strategic manoeuvres with troops to mature current and test futuristic doctrines. Focus: high order of operational fitness of the entire range of weapons and equipment.

I was in the hot seat as a brigadier, heading the repair and recovery organization of the formation. Reliable fleet and weapons infuse confidence in the fighting force. Having taken the preventive maintenance actions in time and integrated the first aid technical teams for support in situ, we were sitting pretty, and itching to be launched. The combat force was reassured to fight unhindered without having to look back. They relied on us, for war-waging capability was directly proportional to the fitness of the fleet. Trigger: the confidence earned by our teams of the supported arms.

The numbers matter when it comes to the actual weapons and equipment available in road worthy condition in the hands of the troops. This is exactly what our teams were excelling at—keeping the 'out of action state' to near zero.

The nature of operations demanded high technical acumen and an innovative mind. The key was in understanding the existing battlefield scenario, the status of the equipment and the future operational scene. I had a superb team which was spirited and innovative. They gave shape to all our plans. Also, I was pleasantly surprised by the formal recognition of our effort by the chief of the Army staff, who decorated me with his Commendation Card. God! How much I wanted all this to last forever! But it doesn't happen so in higher ranks. Once you have established yourself and are ready to contribute, it is also the time to move on, making way for fresh minds. My case was no different. As soon as the mandatory period ended, I received my marching orders. I was to head the personnel and administration affairs of Eastern Command at the famous Fort William in Kolkata.

I had mixed reactions for my new assignment. Surely the station was good. I had heard much about the beautiful environment and facilities both in Fort William and the metropolis. We were all full of enthusiasm and had great expectations when we reached Kolkata. Unfortunately, our induction and timing of move were ominous. To start with, the reception team lost us in the massive crowd at the Howrah Railway Station. I think the platform had been switched at the last minute. I learnt later that it was a common feature. Climatically, Kolkata was at its worst. It was at the peak of heat and humidity when we reached there. One was constantly perspiring. The sun blazing with all its vengeance and its rays were like hot piercing darts. October to February was pleasant, but it was only May when we arrived. To add to our travails, there was no earmarked accommodation initially, and so we had to rough it out for quite some time. As far as the metropolis was concerned, pot-holed roads, painfully slow traffic, never-ending processions, and road blocks said it all. However, with time, all the negatives were to take a backseat. Camaraderie in Fort William and the spirit and affection of Kolkata grew on us.

As regards my job, it was not even remotely connected to what I was handling in my previous assignments. I had to start on a clean slate. Dealing with the personnel and administrative matters, 'A' matters in the Army parlance, was not so popular. Career officers would avoid such jobs if they could. The job was heavy, driven by rules and regulations, legalistic, ever suspecting, and generally negative in attitude. In short, though handling personnel matters, the personal touch was lacking. In the honour board in my office, none of my predecessors had made it to the next rank. In my case, I was the first one from the technical stream to be posted to this general staff job. I learnt later that a conscious decision had been taken to post career officers to streamline handling of personnel matters including discipline and welfare as these have a vital bearing on the morale of the force. Interestingly, I was the first one on the block.

After initial briefings, I was on my own. Before getting bogged down with the routine, I analysed our charter and set my priorities. First of all, I thought it vital to lift the image of the 'A' branch to that of a humane and an accessible one. Our charter mainly comprised of handling discipline and vigilance matters, D&V in short, welfare of troops and their families, policies of personnel service matters and the medical related cases. Medical facilities and casualty evacuation from the remote areas were sensitive issues and had to be addressed as such. Finally, innocuous but the most relevant matters relating to the ceremonials. Any of the above issues could become hot and emergent at any point of time. I may add that any type of case which did not fall specifically in the domain of operations or logistics would find a way to us. I had forbidden my team to return any case without my having seen it. In short, the buck stopped with us.

Eastern Command was responsible to maintain sanctity of our borders to the north and east, stretching across the states of West Bengal, Sikkim, Assam, Meghalaya. Arunachal Pradesh, Tripura, Mizoram, Manipur and Nagaland. Insurgency was active in many of these states particularly in Assam, Nagaland and Manipur. This gave rise to typical cases of discipline and welfare when security forces were deployed for specific operations in conjunction with the civil administration.

Discipline and vigilance matters were sensitive and time bound. These obviously had to be addressed on top priority. In doing so, we had to ensure that we were ahead of the dead lines and that our fundamental analysis itself was so thorough that the directions or recommendations vested legally in the Army Commander would remain final and none were rescinded or contestable in a court of law. And if contested, the same were appealed against promptly seeking restoration of the decisions. In short, the examination and our recommendations had to be water tight. In addition, there were also many cases of administrative action, which did not fall in the domain of direct disciplinary proceedings but were equally sensitive. We also had to ensure a thorough and professional application of mind before recommending or initiating any disciplinary proceedings. Initiation of a case is like the snout of a glacier. Once an inquiry is initiated, the battle procedure gushes out unbridled. Thereafter, it is not easy to close the case mid-course, there being legal implications. This implied that a large number of personnel, units and formations would get busy in completion of these proceedings. Their entire routine and creative contribution for furtherance of operations would be adversely affected. In finalization of these cases, moving witnesses from all over the country was the key. But it was an extremely tedious process. We had to coordinate this at the apex level. Which we did.

I had a good team of officers. Out of them, only my second level was in the run for promotion, but he was not in the D&V chain. The rest of the officers had already been superseded and many out of them were way senior to me. They had rich experience and knowledge, but also had big ego. They needed recognition of their effort. In short, they needed to be pampered. I fondly called them D&V boys. Once they understood the priorities, they fell in line. Life was smooth thereafter. To monitor all this, I put my information system in place. I had to be meticulous in this monitoring only for a while. Soon the system started working smoothly like a well oiled machine. We were all the time ahead of the deadlines. Our professional examination considerably reduced any repetition or infructuous effort in countering the appeals, because there were none or minimal. What stood out loud and clear was that we had to have courage of conviction in the examination and assessment of any case. One was not to read the commander's mind and tow any party line. We eminently followed this and never allowed the truth to be compromised. Many a time, we had to be at variance with the internal judicial examination keeping the ground conditions in mind. This only led to a healthy and mature decision.

Though there can be no compromise on discipline, but undue alarms also send wrong signals. Imagine, if after years of disciplinary proceedings, nothing worthwhile comes out. Entire hierarchy is embarrassed and some careers and lives ruined in the bargain. One can also imagine the social stigma and the trauma of not only those under investigation but also of their families. In due course, the number of violations resulting in disciplinary cases reduced, as the commanders saw our point. Instead of being trigger happy, they had to look for the indicators and act at the earliest. Aim was to nip the evil in the bud and not allow it to simmer and grow into a volcanic eruption. The message went down the command well. This had a positive bearing on the morale of the troops. I think our recommendations in this regard were well received and implemented. Productivity of my branch had visibly improved. My heart missed a beat when the Army Commander, who was known to be a stickler for perfection and conservative in praise, specifically complimented me for running the branch better than he had ever seen anywhere. Thanking him, with my heart pounding, I pinched myself to check if all this was real. Without any hesitation, I passed the credit down the chain. I sat back reflecting. All this in such a short time?

In the interregnum, I became entitled to a reserved accommodation in Fort William. A portion of the accommodation on the ramparts had been modified for senior officers holding sensitive appointments. I had been catapulted into this elite company, thanks to the review of the policy. The fort had a unique history dating back to 1758 when its construction was conceived as a sequel to capitulation of the old fort to the Nawab of Bengal, Siraj ud-Daulah. The East India Company's expansive designs to transit to armed traders had earned the ire of the Nawab. Improving the fortification of the fort was the trigger. His warnings remained unheeded, as a result of which, he asserted his authority.

He stormed the outpost of Kassim Bazaar in May 1756. The ease with which he succeeded encouraged him to attack the old Fort William ahead of the Company's anticipation. The British were not an organized force, and even the fort was not so defensible. The soldiers capitulated with very little resistance. The governor fled deserting his command. The events that followed saw the British grow in strength and recapture the fort. Thereafter, construction of the present Fort William started and was completed in 1781. By then, the British were in full control of Bengal. The present fort remains a symbol of power of the Raj and the seat of their Bengal Presidency. Interestingly, it was never baptized by fire and not a single shot has been fired at and from this fort. After Independence, though it lost its raison d'être, it continues to house military headquarters responsible for defence of the eastern borders as a sign of our national sovereignty. It was the focal point for control of the entire operations in 1971 resulting in creation of a new country, Bangladesh[1]. The fort was a citadel. Besides the military headquarters, it could house a large number of troops, officers, families, shopping complexes, and recreational facilities. These have been amply modernized and improved over the years. It was, without a doubt, a privilege to live in this glorious complex which boasted of a rich heritage.

Having anchored well on the professional front, it was time to step out and explore this famous city. The most striking observation to an open mind was the need for massive improvement in the infrastructure of the city. The city was bursting at its seems with a population of nearly 4.5 million of which a large percentage were the immigrants with little or no cover on their heads. On the flip side, the most striking observation was the rare degree of patience, the spirit of fellowship and camaraderie, general state of happiness, and visible contentment amongst the inhabitants. No wonder, Kolkata has a rich cultural history. Fine arts like dance, theatre, classical, and light music have flourished there. The literary bend of mind of the people is visible from the popularity of book fairs and rich Bengali literature.

---

1. Extracts summarized from *Fort William: A Historical Perspective*, a collaborative work by Eastern Command, Indian Army and a professional research team, Sankar Mondal, Calcutta.

Kolkata is also called the city of palaces. Much credit for creating rich architectural legacies goes to the British. An amalgam of Gothic art, Roman architecture and Indo-Islamic motifs make a resplendent display in the city. Some of the famous structures include the Victoria Memorial, the National Museum, the National Library, the Dakshineswar Kali Temple, and a host of palaces, offices, and elite educational institutions dotting the city. The fervour of the celebrations surrounding Durga Puja, the most important festival in Kolkata, is inspiring and is a binding factor for the populace. Penchant for fish and sweets like rasogulla and sandesh (sweet yogurt) has given rise to many good eating joints in the city. What makes Kolkata very attractive and livable is its people's fondness for club life. No wonder the city offers a very healthy and affectionate social life where the affluent and middle class rub shoulders without any complexes. Another factor binding the people is football. Thus, 'Kolkatans love football' will be an understatement. They go in frenzy when it comes to witnessing the matches between their favourite rival teams, be it Mohan Bagan or Mohammedan Sporting Club. Hundreds of footballers throng the central lung space of the city, the Maidan, in the mornings and evenings to exercise and play the game. Their respect for the defence forces was disarming. It was not an uncommon sight to see the entire traffic being brought to a standstill to allow a military staff car or a flag vehicle to pass through.

We relished the club life at Fort William. The Officers' Institute was perhaps the most popular institute of all the cantonments and military stations in the country. Its weekly events were attended by all. I credit this single factor to a large extent for maintaining harmonious relationships. Possibly, it did have a bearing on minimal disciplinary cases in the station, thereby indirectly reducing the workload of my branch. Fort William Golf Course had reciprocal arrangements for the members to play golf, with international level golf courses of the city, the most noteworthy being the Royal Calcutta Golf Course. It is the oldest golf course in the country. I had the privilege to win a major amateur tournament on this golf course.

Kolkata was also famous for Mother Teresa and her monumental work for the humanity. She founded the Missionaries of Charity in 1950 in Kolkata and continued to take care of the sick and dying, refugees, ex-prostitutes, abandoned children, lepers, AIDS victims and the aged with her spirit of love and selflessness, irrespective of religion, caste or creed. She had been awarded the Nobel Peace Prize and the highest national civilian honour, the Bharat Ratna, for her services to humankind. She had been keeping unwell for sometime. Her frail body succumbed to a cardiac arrest on 5 September 1997.

The Government of India decided to give her the state funeral, befitting a person of her stature. Being a ceremonious event, the entire responsibility of coordination with the state government and planning and conduct of the proceedings fell in our lap. The magnitude and gravity of this challenge grew by the day. With multiple agencies coming into play, coordination and planning became much complex. To conduct such a mega event, one had to be specific, yet be discreet so as not to tread on any sensibilities. To start with, the body was to lie in state. But for how long? One was not sure. Finally, the date was decided to be 13 September. This was perhaps one of the longest periods for body of such an eminent personality to lie in state. The venue for this was famous St. Thomas Church of Kolkata. We had to swing into action fast.

The body was embalmed and was to lie in state for the public to pay obeisance. The national flag of India was draped ceremoniously on her by six general officers in their full regalia. Thereafter, senior officers stood in vigil round the clock. On the scheduled day, the casket was carried ceremoniously by pall bearers to the gun carriage that was decked with flowers. Throngs of people jostled en route for a last look at the frail body of that great personality. The gun carriage was escorted by the local formation commander with an impressive cavalcade. The funeral mass was attended by heads of the states, queens, first ladies, cardinals, senior delegates from all over the world, besides the who's who of India. After the eulogy by the Cardinal from Vatican, and laying down the wreaths by the dignitaries, the casket was placed again on the gun carriage by the pall bearers. Our formation commander, the escorts and the modified cavalcade moved to the Mother House, peeling off prior to the private burial. The most sensitive aspect of this entire ceremony stretching over eight days was the live coverage by national and international media. All our actions were as if on the ramp. Falling in the wake of similar unfortunate demise of Lady Diana, our task had become much difficult. Comparisons were likely to be drawn. Thanks to the efforts of one and all, I dare say, we did alright.

Notwithstanding the diversions by mega events, my main job continued at the same pace. The back log could not be allowed to pile up. The deadlines still had to be met. I had learnt to take all the pressures in my stride. In spite of an extremely busy and taxing schedule, we were happy and content. Surely, time spent must have been spent well. Before we knew, nearly three years had elapsed. I owe a lot for my personal growth to my years in Fort William. On the family front, our daughter was auspiciously married; our son, an engineer, was admitted to one of the top universities of USA for higher studies. On my personal front, I was approved for promotion to the next rank, to be a Major General, breaking the jinx of my branch. My wife too had come to love the fort life. Later, we moved with nostalgia to the Western Theatre. It was to be yet another sensitive and hot seat on the general staff. I was to head the logistics and administration of Western Command.

9

My Challenges as a Logistician

Logistics in simple terms is planning, procurement, provision, and disposal of all materials and services support to the force in the right quantity, at the right time and at the right place economically and efficiently. A simple statement but a tall order...

Venue: headquarters of Western Command Chandimandir. Agenda: review of the operational situation and fine tuning our response. Forum: operational. Situation: live. Operation Vijay, code name for the Kargil operations already active in the Northern Theater. My agenda: to plan logistics support. The situation under review had arisen on account of covert infiltration from across the border and surreptitious occupation of some of our area by the infiltrators in the highly inaccessible terrain of Kargil sector. Counter-operations had been launched by our Northern Theatre to evict them. As a cautionary measure, we were on the alert and our formations were in a state of operational readiness, poised for an appropriate response if required.

I had moved to the Western Theatre on promotion from Kolkata a few months earlier to head the logistics of this elite force which had crack strike and holding formations on its order of battle. These formations were highly motivated and meticulously trained to exploit full potential of the force. Prime combat component of this force was its massive tank fleet, mechanized infantry and infantry integrally supported by state of the art artillery, engineers, air defence, reliable communications, and a well-knit logistics system. As chief of the logistics, it was my responsibility to plan and ensure integrated logistics support to all the formations so that they could conduct the operations unhindered.

Logistics' support for the Army, commonly understood as administrative support, had a mammoth charter. It encompassed virtually everything in material support and services that the Army needed. Ironically, this aspect of planning and conduct of war had been lesser understood and considered unglamorous not only by us but also by most armies in the world. No wonder this vital part of the Army has been nicknamed 'the tail'. It was a necessary evil, though constantly under the scanner of the Army planners to downsize. Thanks to the continued state of militancy, we have come a long way. There has been a paradigm shift in the attitude of military thinkers. Importance of logistics has been increasingly accepted. Interestingly, I was perhaps the first officer from technical services stream to have been entrusted with this sensitive and operational appointment.

Logistics in simple terms encompass planning, procurement, provision, and disposal of all materials and services which support the Army in the right quantity, at the right time and at the right place economically and efficiently. The canvas is very wide and the job nightmarish. For ease of my comprehension,

I subdivided my responsibility into four distinct segments. As I analysed each one of these, the efforts involved and the priority each one of these deserved crystallized.

First, operational logistics. This involved providing logistics support to the entire force during the operations, and integrating them with the higher logistics chain at the Army and national level. I found operational logistics to be the most interesting part of my responsibility. It dealt with live situations. The system was well set and responsive. It was, by and large, flexible at the tactical level of operations. However, at the strategic level, one had to create infrastructure well in advance, failing which large-scale changes in plans would either not be possible or would require a logistical pause in the operations. With time, I was able to get a consensus on the creation of requisite infrastructure. It gave us tremendous flexibility.

It was vital to gain confidence of the formations in the logistical chain. Once assured, the demands dropped to realistic levels. This helped in curbing the tendency to seek more provisions than required, thereby releasing uncalled for pressures on the procurement chain. I considered it vital for the staff not to personalize the powers delegated to them; they were to be facilitators and were expected not to hold back resources which were due forward. My experience as an instructor of logistics in the Army War College and my tenure in a strike formation gave me a head start. In actual execution, what made the difference was the positive attitude and dedication of our team.

Second, provision of infrastructure; also called 'works' in the Army parlance. This included maintenance and development of the existing infrastructure and creation of additional infrastructure in the entire theatre to include various cantonments and military stations. The infrastructure included all types of accommodation including office, living, storage, and allied facilities. The storage accommodation was vital particularly for logistical depots. Ammunition storage required highly specialized accommodation. We had to cover a lot of ground in this aspect. Execution of the works was carried out under the aegis of our engineers. Finally, acquisition of land and hiring of accommodation, if necessary, in conjunction with the defence estates agency at various echelons. I found this part of my responsibility to be the most tedious and time consuming. Pitiably, the system, though vital for the Army, was not too responsive; its main impact was visible only in the long term. The procedures were too long and bureaucratic. There was a long gestation period from the proposal stage to implementation on ground. One needed a sharp eye, otherwise much could go undetected till it would be too late to alter.

Ironically, major projects seldom take off during one's tenure, so one did not get the satisfaction of seeing his efforts actually taking shape. Most commanders wish to improve local facilities much faster than the procedures permit, but this gives rise to conflicting situations. We found that maximum defaults were occurring in the execution of the works. An elaborate monitoring system was put in place. This helped us in seeking accountability. With time, the message was driven home and the pressure eased when results started showing well in time. What mattered was motivation of the staff and recognition of the executing agencies, which always remained at the receiving end in spite of their sustained efforts.

Third was personnel management. This included all aspects dealing with the in-service phase of the personnel, discipline and vigilance, ceremonials, terms and conditions of service, welfare and so on. Out of these, discipline and vigilance and ceremonials needed a close watch. Welfare assumed much greater importance following the Kargil operations. Discipline and vigilance, which normally would have accounted for maximum time otherwise, was my direct responsibility in my previous assignment in the Eastern Theatre where the conditions were far more trying. Further, the environment prevailing in this part of the country did not generate many complicated cases. Therefore, I had that much of an edge. Needless to say, each case still had to be thoroughly understood and this required time and priority as the cases were time bound.

Finally, coordination; with various service elements of the logistics, with the formations vertically up and down, horizontally with other theatres, with the state governments, and other departments of the central government like defence accounts, audit, defence lands, etc. I considered this as the most vital part of my charter. Each major logistics service at the theatre headquarters was headed by a two-star general. Coordination with the civilian counterparts was yet another game of equations. Interpersonal relations and communication had to be responsive to the sensitivities of one and all. Harmony and goodwill were our main focus for smooth functioning of this complicated chain. There was no scope for creating any friction, yet efficient functioning and accountability could not be compromised. Need to keep the ego under the carpet could not be overemphasized. Ironically, many cases get delayed or don't take off because the key functionaries don't talk to each other and demystify the impediments or maintain a hidden agenda. I realized that openness and transparency in dealings was the only way to get through any mental blocks. This tenet lends dignity to interaction and leads to healthy relationships. Every one then realizes that they are part of the same team. They find ways and means to make the agenda a success. I loved this part of my charter and made many lasting relationships from these official interactions.

Kargil operations gave us a unique opportunity to shake off the shackles of lethargy which tends to set in if tranquility prevails for too long. Many cobwebs in our procedures were removed, and many aspects which tend to be swept under the carpet during exercises due to massive effort and finances involved were addressed headlong. All stages of operational logistics were thoroughly tested. A rare level of enthusiasm was in the air. Spirit of the rear area establishments, that is, the logistic installations located well behind but directly supporting the formations deployed forward, to reach out in support of the forward echelons was amazing. The will and commitment at all levels brought the entire system of logistics together. The end result was that all our formations including their weapons and equipment were well poised for their operational roles.

Another major fallout of Kargil operation was that need was felt for refinement of our casualty evacuation system, upgradation of our medical facilities, due recognition to the martyrs and the wounded, and impact on their families. This brought the aspect of welfare of troops in the limelight. The media brought this operation live to the drawing rooms of the common man. Live coverage of the ceremonious last rites of the martyrs, interviews of their parents, widows and their children, and their spirit made the system rethink about the paltry compensations awarded to them. There was a sudden surge in the will to take better care of the war casualties and their families, and to help them rehabilitate and lead a dignified life. Ex gratia compensations from the central government and our own welfare funds were substantially enhanced and formalized. Most of the state governments too came forward for similar compensations. Perhaps the biggest gain of this operation was that it revived the national bonding with renewed vigour.

Next to the operations, the most challenging situation that we faced was the flash floods in River Satluj which virtually wiped out a major part of our logistical garrison in the northern sector. Lashing rains must have damaged a dam, resulting in the deluge. Water gushed out with unprecedented force, the level rose suddenly, and the wave front, as high as 35 feet, moved with speed like a monster, wiping out everything which came its way. All this happened in the middle of the night. Thanks to a daring helicopter pilot of our Air Force, I landed there at the earliest opportunity to take a stock of the damage. The garrison was cut off for a while. Maintaining the garrison and restoration of the facilities was a mammoth task, but was done in record time by tremendous effort of one and all, including the able support of our Air Force. In short, there was no dearth of challenges. What mattered was the spirit and attitude of our team. Their dedication and hard work made them winners in my eyes.

One would think that if everything was so smooth, then where was the nightmare? In hindsight, I realize that it was not so simple after all. Tremendous amount of toil and effort had been put in to achieve what our team did. We had learnt that it was easier to be positive and take on the challenges in our stride. Functioning becomes much easier thereafter. Whatever be the pressures and challenges, there was never a dull moment for us. I was in this chair for nearly three years, witnessing many major events and changes in the command which was quite rare for such a busy and sensitive appointment.

On my personal front, once the professional pressure eased, I took time to look at Chandimandir military station and the facilities that it offered. Perched in the folds of the foothills of the Shivaliks, Chandimandir military station is a lush green stretch. Dotted with a large variety of trees and flora and fauna in addition to the natural Kikar trees and other berry bushes, it heartily supports a variety of wildlife. Thanks to the lavish plantation of trees, this station enjoys cooler ambience and much higher rainfall than its neighbouring cities. Our bungalow was situated right in the lap of the nature, hidden in a grove of pine trees. The serene environment and the peaceful ambience gave it a feel of a hill station. We fell in love with this place at the first sight. All this led to our decision to settle down in its vicinity after my retirement. The marriage of our son during this tenure marked another benchmark in our life. In terms of extracurricular activities, my squash continued unabated. I also had the privilege to score a hole in one at the scenic golf course of Chandimandir. This feat was later replicated by our son. Like earlier, this tenure was only a precursor to yet another challenging job which was to be in the operational area in the Northern Theatre.

10

My Last Fling

Life is but a chase of fleeting opportunities; The opportunities ever elusive, but these are there for sure...

We had been driving for sometime along the steady but treacherous climb through the narrow valley on our way from TangTse to the southeastern part of Ladakh bordering Tibet. Overlooking the valley were steep and rocky mountains on both sides; running parallel, too steep and too close for comfort. It was like moving through a deep gorge. The imposing ridgelines seemed in complete control of the entire scene. The snow-capped mountains were looking down with disdain, hardly allowing the sun rays to penetrate, and casting long and eerie shadows. The opening between the ridgelines was too narrow, appearing to be narrower still at the top; leaning over, as if threatening to merge, engulfing everything below. Except for the hissing sound of the wind, a scary and an uneasy calm prevailed in the entire valley. Once out of the meandering roads of the mountainous terrain, easing into the stretch of plains was a great relief. We could hardly have imagined what lay ahead.

Suddenly, we were exposed to the most breathtaking view beyond our wildest imagination. A massive lake, most beautiful in its turquoise blue azure, looking as if a giant sapphire was lying prostrate in contrast to the majestic stretch of the desert unfolding astride. It seemed as if both stretched till the end of the horizon and beyond. This captivating view held us mesmerized. It was a rare combination of the two extreme types of terrains coexisting; one devoid of water and the other nothing but water. Ironically, the water is brackish; it is neither potable nor does it support marine life.

As if this was not enough, the colour of the water changed every few kilometres astride the shore from deep blue to emerald green to garnet amber and so on. The shades of each colour deepened with the lateral distance from the shore—a visual grandeur made possible by the reflection of the garnet hills overlooking both sides of the lake. This multi-chromatic extravaganza of the nature was both a feast and test of our ocular faculties. This was the famous lake Pangong Tso, located in the strategic area of southeastern Ladakh at a height of nearly 14,000 feet above the sea level, stretching over 130 kilometres, with nearly two-thirds across the border into Tibet. This area has a history of rare valour of our troops during the Indo-Chinese conflict of 1962. This was just one spectacle of the type of terrain we had to confront in the Northern Theatre. The area is replete with yet higher and tougher reaches. I was on my first visit, having recently taken over as the head of the repair and recovery organization of the Northern Theatre of the Indian Army.

The Northern Theatre had unique challenges. It was responsible for a vast stretch of our border including the entire state of Jammu and Kashmir. The area of responsibility comprised of virtually every type of terrain conceivable. These were open country, riverine, semi-mountainous, mountainous, high altitude, super high altitude, the elevated desert of Ladakh, and finally, the glacial area of Siachen. Each of these stretches had a different connotation. The entire border was operationally active, with sporadic firing of small arms and mortars along the line of control and regular artillery fire exchanges in the glacial area. The glacier area had heights ranging above 21,000 feet above the sea level. Survival itself was a unique challenge there. The line of actual control was relatively quiet but it had its share of stray incidences of border patrol skirmishes with claims and counter claims. Rugged mountainous terrain and thick forested areas of the high altitudes facilitated infiltration of terrorists trained across from our west. The terrorists disrupted the movement in the interior lines and melted into the thick forests in the hinterland, making the entire region war-like. In short, the situation was live and operationally active both on the borders and interior areas. The scenario was of an undeclared war.

The role of my organization was to provide repair and recovery cover to the weapons and equipment held by the combat and support elements in the Northern Theatre and maintain these in a high state of operational fitness at all times. Due to the large variety of terrains, the range of weapons and equipment suited for such terrains too was high. This made our job more difficult. In view of the vast stretch of the borders, and the limitations imposed by each type of terrain, it crystallized that the formations had to be supported for repair and recovery by their integral organizations which were equipped and trained accordingly. These were strengthened by higher technical echelons, some within the vicinity and the rest in the rear. All these elements had to be focussed for a high order of operational preparedness of the weapons and equipment with the troops all the time. Thus we evolved customized repair techniques to reduce the time the equipment or weapon was lying out of action for repairs to the minimum. Our underlying aim was to take the burden off the combat echelons so that they did not have to look over their shoulders. In doing so, we had to overcome many constraints, including shortfall of some vital spares, diagnostic equipment and technical expertise for high-tech weapons and systems at a given point of time. For this, we had to integrate the effort at various levels including the defence-oriented installations and the industry in the rear.

To our pleasant surprise, they all were too willing to be integrated in this chain. They became our extended family, throwing all bureaucratic hurdles out of the window. Lack of spares was not to deter or delay the repairs; innovation was encouraged to make the weapon or equipment functional even partially, if not in full, till proper spares were arranged. In short, no effort was left unturned to speed up the repairs. The principles and techniques that we followed were not new; we only defined these precisely, held deliberations at various echelons, anlaysed the pros and cons, eliminated ambiguity if any, coordinated with sister organizations involved and the command channel, and made these work. Although it appeared simple, it was easier said than done.

In order to make our efforts a success, we had to face many challenges headlong. Some of these included catering for a plethora of contingencies which emerged due to a large variety of the terrain, multiple options, tactical contingencies, and a wide variety of weapons and equipment. The variety of weapons and equipment ranged from tanks to snow scooters, artillery guns, small arms, surveillance equipment, radars, radio communication equipment, vehicles and so on. Each of these varieties, in turn, had a wide range suitable for each type of terrain. This required a detailed analysis of each type of weapon and equipment, the commonality of spares, the test equipment, the skills required, and positioning these accordingly. We felt that it was vital to enhance our technical competence, particularly of young tradesmen. Keeping in view the profile of our technical manpower, this was undertaken on war footing. The next factor we had to counter was to reduce the delays imposed by restrictions on the movement. Due to terrorist activities in the rear, internal movement had to be regulated. The lines of communications in the forward zones were invariably sanitized. We countered this delay by creating a bank of modules, spares and expertise, and positioning these innovatively.

Yet another challenge was the delay caused by the need for acclimatization in the high altitudes. We countered this as well to the best of our ability. Proliferation of weapons and equipment posed the biggest challenge for the spares, which could hardly be positioned in penny pockets all over. Statistical analysis helped us to categorize these spares, and we tried to meet vital requirements; for the rest, innovation was the order of the day. Lastly, we had to bring an attitudinal change in our technical manpower. Their effort in keeping the tanks rolling, the guns firing and the communication networks functional was a direct contribution in the war effort. They had to be recognized as such. It was our responsibility to make them feel as vital cogs in the wheel and not just those who also ran. This was to be our main challenge. For this, we had to strengthen our junior leadership, delegate the powers of technical decisions appropriately and project them in a befitting manner. It was heartening to see a sea change in the functioning of our technical personnel. They were soon beaming with pride and bursting with confidence.

As the saying goes, success begets success. Even minor successes were sufficient to inspire our young teams operating in the hot war environment, be it in support of the force on the line of control or sanitizing the line of communication, or deployed on the Siachen Glacier, the roof of the world. They functioned day and night, unmindful of their personal comfort and safety, spurred by the fire in the belly. They continued to shine with their enthusiasm unabated. Some of their achievements were beyond even our comprehension. Their performance was amazing. All they needed was a trigger. We were to learn with pride that some of the vital mechanized vehicles that had become unreliable due to aging were upgraded in situ and from within the available resources in an inaccessible area. Creation of such facilities and that too so quickly in the back of the beyond was something rare. They brought glory to one and all. It was heartening to learn that some of our vital equipment, essential to support the Siachen operations, lying out of action for quite some time for want of spares, were repaired innovatively, even without the original spares having materialized, in record time.

In yet another case, it was my privilege to announce that two of our young armament experts, including one officer, had dived into River Indus to retrieve a few components from an artillery gun, which had fallen off a precarious landslide in the river a few years earlier and was beyond retrieval. With these components, two guns already deployed were put back in action overnight. Also, in another case, one of our officers with his team was instrumental in devising a counter to the explosive devices controlled by remote, also called IEDs, Improvised Explosive Devices, commonly planted by terrorists to disrupt road communications. There were numerous cases of initiative and technical innovation all over in the Theatre. It would be a mammoth task to recount all.

Last but not the least, I must mention about the yeoman service rendered by our integral base workshop. It created numerous additional high-tech facilities and improved its productivity by creating a capability beyond any stretch of imagination. It was a matter of pride that this concerted effort of one and all synergized exponentially, resulting in perhaps the highest ever state of operational preparedness of our weapons and equipment.

Although busy, I enjoyed every bit of my tenure in this hot seat. I loved to move out all the time and be at the scene of action. In doing so, I had the privilege to visit each and every sensitive operational area and thus had first-hand experience of the requirements of the combat elements. It helped me to assess the performance of the weapons and equipment better and initiate remedial actions much faster. A large number of issues would be resolved on the spot. This helped us immensely in focussing on what was actually required at the cutting edge. It made our job much easier to translate it to our teams. I was fortunate to head a spirited team. They were technically competent, eager to learn and bubbling with enthusiasm to find solutions. Innovative spirit had become their second nature. The word 'not possible' had disappeared from their dictionary. Recognition of one would become a source of inspiration for many. Heading such a team was indeed a great privilege. I had to relearn the meaning of selflessness from them. I drew inspiration from them rather the other way around. I would often remind myself to keep my wits about, to stay fresh, and keep my thinking faculties intact.

On personal front, I had a wonderful tenure in this station. We had a beautiful and huge bungalow which used to be an Officers' Institute at one time. End to end, it extended beyond any house I was familiar with. The verandah imposing, the scene outside breathtaking with the lawns down below, and the snow-capped peak of Patnitop and its magnificent ridgeline in the distance. It was heavenly! A caring family, congenial work environment, a wonderful team, supportive staff, and understanding commanders. What more could have one asked for? To add to it all, in my spare time, I won the squash tournament, both open and veterans, and even scored a hole in one, third of my golfing career, all as a two-star general. It was like cherry on the cake.

I hardly had time to realize that this tenure was to be my last fling in active service of a long and eventful career spanning over nearly four decades. I had the privilege to hang my uniform here in a stride while at work. Thanks to the operational scenario then prevailing, I was working till late even on the eve of my retirement. We couldn't have been more fortunate; walking out tall, clean, head high and physically fit at the end of this long journey. Little did I know that a formal recognition of my humble contribution was on its way in the form of the second highest presidential award for distinguished services, the Ati Vishisht Seva Medal.

11

On Retirement

Life begins at retirement. It is only a continuation of what one could not pursue earlier...

It was a long drive back to the station we had chosen to settle down after my retirement. We both were quiet, not morose, but brooding. Thinking of life ahead. We had planned and prepared well in advance, yet when it actually happened, it gave a different feeling, a feeling of déjà vu. As if this was not the final farewell: farewell to arms, farewell to the way of life; life that one had lived for over four decades; life that had given us some of our most precious moments; life from my formative years, graduating from an adolescent officer cadet to a bubbling young officer and rising high up the ladder of the Indian Army. It was a farewell to this long and successful journey. A journey with lasting memories. It had been an eventful journey with many successes and many failures. But the journey had been very satisfying. It was due to divine mercies that we had come out unblemished, clean, physically fit, and with dignity at the end of this long journey.

Retirement is perceived differently by different people. According to dictionary, 'retirement' is to recede, to withdraw. Some feel it marks the end of employment, some feel it is the end of the world, and others feel it is the beginning of a new life. For some, it is the setting in of old age, for others it may mean beginning of freedom. All these meanings are true and apply perfectly to someone or the other, depending on his psyche, needs, planning, and attitude towards life. In my case, it was a mixed response. Although I did feel nostalgic about the past, I had realized that life in the Army was not a cakewalk. Every day had a challenge of its own. If the operational scene did not keep one busy, some functional challenges would crop up, and if that was not enough, the massive organization one controlled could go awry somewhere, and finally, if nothing else was happening, the persons above you were always there to add spice to life. In short, there was never a dull moment. Keeping this in view, I felt it was time to hang my uniform and be free to control my own time and life. So I viewed retirement as a positive happening. To be free like a bird; to soar and do whatever I wished to. How much of all this would actually happen, time only was to tell.

Retirement may appear too distant when one is young, but this strange phenomenon starts exerting its influence from the very beginning of one's career. Unwittingly, planning for retirement commences alongside the career. All insurances, financial planning and value additions to one's profile are aimed with an eye for the rainy day, albeit post-retirement needs. If one is pragmatic, major benchmarks of life, viz., marriage, children, acquisition of major assets and so on too somehow get linked to the anticipated age of retirement because of finances and energy level. The salary may not be as attractive as the private sector, but the armed forces have a predetermined age of retirement and the government offers pension, though restricted to half the salary. It devolves that one is only partly secure in terms of finance on retirement. Thus, there is a need to plan, invest and even seek a second career if necessary. Notwithstanding all this, one is at least saved from the dilemma of working endlessly, or to decide as to when to call it a day, at what income, or at what level of savings. Notwithstanding the individual's requirements and aspirations, the organizations require to induct fresh blood. Thus, retirement has a meaning for one and all. It only augers that one must prepare and transit to this phase of life with grace. In my case, we had deliberated upon this in depth. I was not only prepared for it, but was secretly looking forward to it.

The most important decision for post-retirement life is to choose the station to settle down. It should be a station which offers facilities for activities of interest, for the anticipated lifestyle, one which suits the budget, has adequate medical facilities, proximity to own kith and kin, and finally, ensures avenues for future employment if the need arises. In the course of my service, Panchkula, the penultimate station of my career, became the obvious choice. After due deliberations, we had acquired a spacious apartment and furnished it according to our liking. Panchkula and the adjoining city of Chandigarh boast of three golf courses within 20 minutes of drive. It is one of the best urban planned cities in the country with spacious roads, large lung spaces and planned markets. It is situated within an earshot of Shimla to the north and New Delhi to the south. With Chandimandir military station in the vicinity as our link to service life, and a large community of retired and serving officer in the area, we found it easy to merge into the environment. We realized that perhaps this was the wisest decision we had taken for ourselves.

Next major issue is of finances. One needs to be able to live with dignity. Anything more is a bonus. I think it is all in the mind and attitude. One's life and lifestyle are bound to undergo a change. If one has not anticipated and is not reconciled to it, then retirement can be traumatic. Moreover, if some major liabilities like acquisition of the dwelling unit, marriage of children, etc., still have to be met, these only add to the challenge. More often than not, budget is the first casualty. If one is not firm and cautious, one is bound to overstretch at the cost of liquidity. One cardinal principle I have always followed is to regulate the expenditure on fixed assets but have adequate liquidity. Liquidity liberates, gives confidence, and a feeling of richness. One may be sitting on high value property, but this value is only notional. Many people plan way ahead and act in time. Initially, I preferred risk-free investments to meet the budget which had many suspense heads. It was a new experience, and a pleasure to monitor this for the first time in my life. Fortunately, I had to do all this only for a short while. A short stint in the corporate world, plenty of dividends from my investment in mutual funds and a few more doses relieved me of this effort thereafter.

Another vital issue is how to be creatively busy after retirement. There are many views on retired life: 'retirement is the world's longest coffee break'; 'challenge of retirement is how to spend time without spending money'; 'money is no better in retirement, but the hours are', 'you don't have to play too much of golf, 18 holes are enough' and so on. Some comic, some pragmatic, and many satirical quotes too have been coined; these may titillate, but the hard truth lurks underneath. Once the sheen of farewell wears off, this truth has to be faced. I faced it on the first morning in our new apartment post retirement. I got up early, got ready, and was instinctively looking for my uniform. That was *the moment*. The moment of truth. I was in a new station, in a new residence, and I was out of service. A very basic question struck me: So what was I to do? All my preparations for this moment started failing me. My daughter, who had graciously joined us to help us ease into new life, aptly handled the situation, saving me from the embarrassment of public display of emotions.

My preparations for retirement also included seeking advice from some of the veterans. I got varying responses to my queries. One said in lighter vein that he had become a go-getter, getting whatever his wife asked him to; another said that it was important to create your own 'O Group'. In the Army parlance, 'O Group' is the short form for Order Group. This group comprises of the commanders of the next tier down the chain. They are given operational orders and are charged with the responsibility to execute the same. This group is your direct command; you control your organization through this group. It gives a feeling of power. In this case, what he meant was that one should have someone to give orders to. Ironically, it turns out the other way. Since wives don't retire, to them one extra hand is now available. Unwittingly, one ends up being in his wife's 'O Group'. The long and short of all is that one has to customize his own routine. This could be an amalgam of time for physical fitness, sports, intellectual and creative pursuits, social circle, finances, and finally shouldering a share of domestic chores. While one gets busy creating a routine for oneself, it is vital to assist the creation of a similar one for the spouse, who too has undergone this change. Ultimate aim of all this is to get a feeling of well being, both physical and mental, and adapt to new way of life.

The last but the most sensitive and important part is to understand the psychological implications. If one has not applied his mind to these, one can be taken off guard. First is the feeling of loneliness which may crepe in. Bereft of any formal organization, one feels that he is on his own. In an anxiety to seek company, some overindulge in social activities, or affiliate themselves to various organizations at the cost of their valuable time and even their identity.

Next, is the tendency to seek recognition and therefore develop an urge to prove themselves. It does not imply that one should not pursue what one wishes to, but it need not be with a feeling of complex. Such a tendency is only reflective of a self-imposed identity crisis.

Finally, it is a common practice for many veterans to don the mantle of experts and analysts overnight, making observations and offering lofty suggestions on matters which they themselves may have failed to deliver, or did not have the courage to point out when in the chair. This can impress only the naïve. Sharing one's expertise and experiences creatively is different from public airing of sermons or criticism. This is not only counter productive but may reflect on their own credibility. In essence, one has to accept the hard reality of life: one has had his innings. It is time to allow the next players to take the strike. Only if one could learn to fade away, it would be dignified and graceful to retire and be a veteran.

Equipped with the above mentioned thoughts, I was ready to analyse how my wife and I had responded to my retirement. Before I could do so, I found myself to be the subject of a case study by many more. In my case, having been very busy and dynamic, many were curious to observe me handle this phase of life. They wondered how I would accept retirement. Would I stagnate, or be depressed, bereft of all powers and attendant responsibilities, or would lack of formal routine tell upon me; would I still be as dignified without all the brass flashing on my shoulders and so on? One of my elder colleagues couldn't help being vocal about it. He took it upon himself to observe me closely for a while. He didn't have to wait too long. Finding no change in us, he graciously took me off his scanner.

In reflection, I too wondered how we had pulled it off so smoothly. It still surprises me how we took the retirement in our stride and adapted to new life like fish takes to water. I feel mental preparation was the key. Attitude towards life was another factor. We believed in transparency in our behaviour and relationships. This made life simple. One was generally content and somewhat detached from what could have been or should have been. This is the mantra for inner happiness for all times and not only during retirement. Initially finances were just about adequate, but still we maintained sufficient liquidity. We kept our major expenditures under control, but were lavish with day-to-day expenditures. This gave us financial freedom. It also reinforced my decision of not taking up a second career. Once we settled down, I was convinced of the need to control my own time and to pursue my life the way I wanted.

It was well deserved after such a long stint in the Army. My interest in outdoor activities strengthened by literary pursuits clinched the issue. Mere sports or social gatherings would give me only a feeling of hollowness. The key activities had to be creative. I would even feel guilty for wasting too much time on golf, though I love this sport, or partying for that matter. Besides reading voraciously, there was also an urge to keep abreast with the latest news and reviews so as to remain updated. We joined a few social groups including a regimental one. This took care of our social needs. We love to travel, or rather drive. I love to visit my hometown, to my moorings, and refresh relationships and recapitulate the memories of my early years. We often visit our children. Ironically, they too have taken upon us, for better or worse. I could not create my 'O Group', but narrowly escaped becoming a go-getter. My wife's independence for movement and my habit of being lavish in purchases tipped the balance in my favour. Our doting pet, a golden Labrador, gained maximum from my retirement. She found a full-time attendant in me. Her disarming gestures and innocent but questioning looks keep me fettered firmly to the terra firma.

Keeping all these in mind, I have devised a routine for myself, compressing most of the above activities in a day, sans any pressure. My wife too got busy with her routine which keeps her creatively occupied. She invariably joins me to the gym in the evenings for a workout. I am fortunate to continue with golf and squash. I mean both on the same day. My passion for books has been a great source of motivation and learning all along. This has only intensified ever since. It is great fun. Books are like friends, live and talking. To top all this, is my latest urge to pen my thoughts, thoughts on life, and on my experiences. This has become the greatest passion for me. It keeps my mind soaring. It has added spice to my life.

I do not really know how time flies. So here we are fairly deep into my retirement, yet getting generous compliments for looking youthful, and with no time to spare, or for any need for escapades. That much for my retirement.

Section-II

My Thoughts

12

On Youthfulness

Psychologically, you are only as old as you think.

-Deepak Chopra

It had been raining incessantly. Dark clouds and murky weather had been our companion the entire day. One did enjoy the platter of rain on the sloping roofs in this beautiful hill station, but what irked us was that the lashing rain had forced us all indoors. Even the birds and animals had to seek some shelter. Life appeared to have come to a standstill. Everyone was waiting as if imprisoned. Animals were waiting to step out and fend for their feed. Fortunate ones like us were waiting to stretch out in the lush green and relish the resplendence and bounty of the nature. Finally, the rain decided to take pity on all and subsided. The clouds started lifting, and the sun struggled to surface in bits and pieces. Sun rays managed to pierce through the retreating canopy of clouds, reflecting at askew angles from the wet leaves of freshly bathed trees. All this presented an exclusive spectacle of beauty extraordinaire.

Slowly, movement started and people started filling the barren streets. The valley had sprung to life. Thanks to this respite, our conversation on a philosophic though catchy topic too was disrupted, and put on hold for the time being. I got a breather; kind of saved by the gong. I had become the target to explain the whys and hows of the wonderful phenomenon of youthfulness as if I had captured it by design. Reason: I had been accused of looking younger than my years, and for no fault of mine. As if I had an access to a secret formula! I had no answers readily available. Neither had I ever applied my mind to this nor had I even realized if it mattered at all. Either way, it was only a gift of nature with a fine print of 'conditions apply', albeit it could be withdrawn with or without notice. Ironically, nature only came to my rescue. It was time to go deeper into this intriguing and ever-fleeting phenomenon; what exactly is youthfulness and why the desire to defy the natural process of aging?

Simply put, youthfulness implies a feeling of being young, of well being, glow on the face, flat stomach, taut skin, bundles of energy, smart looks, sexual vigour, eternal peace with self, and longevity. It follows that fortified with these attributes, one feels enabled to look at life differently and enjoy the pleasures far more and far longer. One feels reassured of oneself and less vulnerable to the cycle of withering away of the body due to the aging process. As a result, one can lead a robust lifestyle, pursue one's passions with vigour, put in untiring and sustained effort and yet feel fresh. Extended to a society, this can be a boon to the humanity and provide improved efficiency and productivity. What more can one wish for? The adage 'health is wealth' is perhaps the ultimate statement that holds true for all living beings. It is not a mere quote, but has a deep impact on our life and lifestyle. The moment one is unhealthy, nothing else really matters. During the phase of the ailment, one's total focus keeps shifting back to the pain and misery. Any amount of diversions in the form of culinary lavishness, luxurious ambience, pecuniary abundance, love, romance and so on fail to inspire. Life becomes dull and drab. One tends to recede into a cocoon and instinctively operates in the default mode of misery.

Longevity is distinct from youthfulness but is commonly implied as a corollary to it. Historically, the need for this can be traced down the continuum of time. In the ancient times, many ascetics have tried to find answers through penance. Some came quite close to achieve immortality till their own arrogance on account of the supernatural powers so acquired resulted in their undoing. Even during the Vedic period and through the era of our epics of *Ramayana* and *Mahabharata*, many kings and sages are known to have worshipped Lord Shiva and Vishnu, the gods who control the cycle of life and death according to Hindu mythology, with the sole aim of seeking a boon of immortality. Many even experimented with tantric *vidya* and imposed extreme ritualistic restrictions and sacrifices on themselves to achieve immortality. During the Medieval Ages, the alchemists worked on this to extract the elixir of life. Galactic impacts and predictions exploring the unorthodox fields of numerology, palmistry and astrology too have been exploited to assess possibilities of attaining longevity and healthy life.

In the modern era, the approach has been more realistic and pragmatic. Extensive scientific research and statistical studies have been undertaken, and analyses carried out with a view to get to the bottom of this intrigue. It may suffice to say that the urge for prolonged youthfulness is universal in nature and has been a known and cherished desire of one and all. But the question remains, how to achieve it, if at all one can?

Modern era offers a plethora of facilities and tools which were unthinkable earlier. Massive strides in medical science have made it possible to change human organs, locate the diseased part and repair it with precision. Research on the stem cells and genetic modification has opened new vistas to slow down the aging process. Preventive medicines enhance immunity and therefore reduce vulnerability to many killer diseases. All this has led to a sharp rise in the average life expectancy. In some European countries, it is as high as 80 years. Would it be fair to infer that adequate longevity has been achieved in such cases? It is ironic to note that although the average life may have increased, the aging process has accelerated rather than declined.

Modern lifestyle, though luxurious, has attendant problems; the most dangerous being competition. Pitifully, this phenomenon starts from infancy and carries on lifelong. As an infant, one is always taught skills ahead of his/her age; as a student one is always busy learning more than his peers and his potential; as an adult, one feels threatened all the time and therefore remains engrossed in his profession. Result: one continues to move fast and forgets to live the life that he ought to. Life becomes too mechanical. One is in constant need of escapades. All this leads to stress of a complex variety; stress generated by peer group, by family, by teachers, by society, in the work environment, by friends, by excess of riches or lack of it, and many self-imposed ones like loneliness, fixation, attitude, lack of confidence and so on. Cumulative effect of all these may lead to premature graying, early loss of hair, pot belly, sunken cheeks, indigestion, diabetic tendency, hypertension, cardiac disorder, lack of glow and energy, etc. Young and middle ages are more vulnerable to them. Thus, the management of all these too starts early. One may sustain and continue for long but the youthfulness withers away. Once the realization dawns, it is either too late or one is past the prime. In short, one has to start young.

Interestingly, challenges throw up opportunities. Awareness of need to remain fit and look young too is increasing by the day. This need is being fully exploited commercially by targeting specific age segments. The media has swamped this theme, health and nutrient-oriented literature has mushroomed, joggers' parks and gymnasia have come up in plenty, many specialized therapies have come up guaranteeing loss of weight, etc. Spas, nature therapy, mud packs, oil massages and what not form a part of tourism itinerary. Yoga has finally been pulled out of the wraps, and what sage Patanjali gave us millenniums back for free is being customized as a novelty in a commercial style. Textile, garment, sports goods, and footwear industries too have stepped in a big way to extract their share of the pie. Customized apparel and footwear are essential for every separate event of this entire exercise. Nutrition science is a new subject which has come up with alternate energy potions in the form of vitamin foods. Even medical science has made forays in 'vigour enhancers' and cosmetic surgery to alter the looks as a shortcut to youthfulness. In short, awareness has been adequately created, the need generated and well marketed. One is prepared to spend to achieve good health and youthfulness. It set me thinking. Was this phenomenon restricted to only those who could afford it? And what model had I followed? The fog was disappearing. The mystery started unravelling. It was a eureka moment. I was now ready to continue with the disrupted conversation.

First, some revealing myths and realities about youthfulness. It is a reality that there is no such disease or phenomenon called youthfulness that our modern medical science claims to infuse or prolong. They have not yet set their sights on it. It is a myth that young looks automatically imply longevity. The biological clock is ticking all the time, although one may look young physically and feel young psychologically. There is no prescription or manual to achieve youthfulness. One, therefore, cannot work for it. Extensive workout and sports may make a person physically fit, but youthfulness may not follow. There are many top level sportspersons in the peak of their physical fitness but are prematurely gray, bald, ill tempered, and ever discontent. They certainly do not appear youthful. Also, youthfulness cannot be acquired off the shelf. Therefore, it is not the forte of the 'haves' only. What perhaps emerges is that youthfulness is an intrinsic phenomenon, and its source is purely internal, though external activities may help.

In my perception, one has to view life as a whole. One has to learn to love life and enjoy every moment of it. For this, one has to be at peace with the self, seek and practice the truth, be pure at heart, be simple and straightforward, be transparent in interpersonal interactions, be humane and full of compassion, have honesty of purpose, and be content with what one gets. All these aim solely at seeking intrinsic happiness. All these are basic tenets; these are natural to the young, but we tend to drift away with age. What is required is to reign in the urge to violate these basic tenets. Developing self control is the key for this, but it is tough to achieve.

Here are some basic facts of life, which may help in developing self control. No situation in life is ideal. Life is a zero sum game. In every situation, one gains some and loses some. Maybe the time domains are different. Therefore, there are no clear winners or losers. In the continuum of life, there is no distinct boundary between pleasure and pain. There is sufficient overlap where both are present in varying degrees. Fortified with these facts, one may infer that even by violating the basic tenets, one may not gain finally, but definitely lose out in the long run. On the contrary, the reverse could be equally true. If that be so, why not take the better option? I was ready to put myself on the block for self analysis.

In my case, the test to meet the challenge of violating the basic tenets of life came very early. I recall when I was 16 and had various options in front of me to join any of the top engineering institutions, one of my revered elders confronted me with a searching question. He bluntly asked me if I would make money on the side, which was a known practice then. My prompt and reflexive response was no. Thereafter, it became my commitment to myself which I wanted to honour lifelong. This single incidence influenced my way of looking at life. Later, I only kept extending this thought to my complete lifestyle. My confidence in values continued to be reinforced with time. I realized that idealism was no longer a dream. One could at least attempt to head in that direction. This became a source of inspiration to me. I was able to grow with impunity, but many others were stalled in their growth and were left out. But then this is the cost one has to be prepared to pay. You don't lose it all, you gain somewhere. In short, if you can walk your talk, your mind is at peace. There is no complication. Life becomes simpler and no façade is required. Once the ground rules were in place, all that I had to do was to devise a routine integrating profession, sports, and my hobbies. But all these were to be mutually inclusive.

Fortunately, fitness has been a fad for me. Therefore, sports, workouts, yoga, etc., have been like my second nature. In my busy professional life, it was not possible to accommodate all these, but I could always find time and way for something. Sweating out was a must. That helped me remain fit and enjoy good health and love life. It also kept me away from many infructuous distractions. In my professional life, there was no compromise when it came to competence, values, integrity and loyalty to the cause. All this could be even at the cost my own furtherance. I had ambitions, but was not ambitious. Therefore, the targets were pitched at the level of my potential and were achievable. These were always short term. I could not and did not want to see too far ahead. I wanted to enjoy my work and life. Financially, life was not luxurious but we managed with dignity. Some shortage has a charm of its own. One has something to look forward to. I don't claim to be a philanthropist, but am definitely concerned when it comes to those who are deprived.

This attitude has helped me immensely in my family life. My children developed values of life, worked hard and in turn have become my role models. I had developed the habit of reading early in life. This has been the biggest asset for me. I was never alone, and there has never been sufficient time in a day. All that I have done is to weave my routine around the activities mentioned above and have tried not to dilute the values so dear to me. Consequently, I am at peace, and I am content and busy. There has been no effort to work for or seek youthfulness. Even having retired for some time, I have deliberately not opted for a second career because I wanted to live my life my way. During all this, the benign hand of nature still continues to be in my favour, and I continue to be accused of looking younger than my age. This model is available for the asking. But I offer no guarantees, because I myself have none.

13

On Love

Love is a many-splendoured thing...
-Buddy Adler's movie (1955)

It was a bright starry night. The sky was surprisingly clear. The ever-hanging pollution had been washed down by the rain. The nearly full moon had risen early, adding to the splendour of the night. It stood majestically in the dark sky; very bright and shining. Its silvery light was reflecting on the vast expanse of water. The tidal waves rising; yearning for a mere touch of their paramour, the moon. The beach was very tranquil except for the splashing sound of the waves that were playing hide and seek with the sea shore. Water running up, inundating everything en route, and then receding; only to return with renewed vigour. Lights of the distant ships twinkling as if the celestial bodies had swooped down not to be left out of this extravaganza. Overall, the ambience was out of the world, very soothing, very personal, very poetic, and very romantic. The setting was ideal for love; love for nature, romance. Overwhelmed by the ambience, I sat there dreaming. Dreaming of love.

I wondered what caused such a feeling of love. This stirred my mind to think 'what exactly is love'? Is it merely an archaic definition in the dictionary: warm affection, attachment, liking or fondness for a thing or a person? Or is it only an emotional display? What causes it and for whom is it meant? Is it to fulfill some material need or is it for a person? Is it a romantic feeling only for the beloved, or for the creator, for parents, children, friends, or one's own self? All these thoughts flashed across my mind.

I felt foolish. Such a common and universal phenomenon, so natural to living beings, yet I had never applied my mind to understand it deeper. Ironically, before this, I had never even cared to look for its formal meaning in the dictionary. How could one be so casual about such a wonderful feeling, the purest emotion perhaps? Or did one take it for granted, or was too confident to experience it, little realizing that everyone may not be as blessed to experience it, leave alone understand its pain and pleasure and the attendant complexities.

As I deliberated, many more associated issues kept emerging. Is love a commitment; is it a one-way traffic; can it exist if not reciprocated; is it a feeling of possession; is it physical; can it be platonic; is it spontaneous or reflexive or a deliberately chosen option; is it mere longing; is it passion or infatuation; is it really blind; does it occur at first sight; and a plethora of such queries started churning up in my mind. Such a simple and natural emotion, yet so complex. No precise answers were forthcoming.

The most common and obvious association of 'love' conjures an emotional attraction between two adults of opposite sexes. So much has been written on this form of love, its purity, intensity, passion, and selflessness. History is replete with many examples of lovers who broke all barriers, sacrificed everything, at times, even their life for love. However, this concept of love has adopted some variations. It may no longer be restricted to opposite sexes, and also the age of either party is no bar. But the essence still remains the same. It is the care and concern for each other and sex may or may not form part of it.

Once in love, nothing else matters to the persons involved, and when it is responded, life takes on a whole new meaning and is blissful. They think only about each other, dream about each other, see each other in everything, adore each other, and perceive each other to be perfect and flawless. Only their love really matters to them. They are in a state of trance. Happy and content. Oblivious to everything else, the lovers are in a world of their own. But the path of love is not simple. Soon, many external forces start mobilizing against them. They won't let the lovers be. How could they? After all, the story won't be complete without their villainous ways. These external forces would include some who are jealous, some who are self-styled custodians of morality and those who derive sadistic pleasure in exercising their powers to dominate the life of others. It makes the lovers' life challenging and interesting. If it was a smooth sailing, how would the pangs of love surface, how would the depth of love be tested, how would the intensity of love reach its epitome, and how would all this be expressed. It may be in the form of lyrics, art, music, literature, anger, anguish, in mere silence of acquiescence, or of surrender to the barriers of caste, creed, society, religion, borders, etc. The outcome of all loves therefore may or may not result in communion. For some, there is pleasure in suffering; the suffering of separation. It keeps the charm alive. For some, it may become the *raison d'être* of life. Perhaps, the separation becomes a source of inspiration.

There are many more facets of love. One of them is love for the creator. It could be practised externally by deeds and worship, while living in the material world or internally by renouncing all material things and undertaking penance for revelation of the Lord. This form may not be akin to interpersonal love. Thus, to call it love may be euphemistic. It is more like devotion. However, there are many examples where the devotees chose to perceive this as interpersonal love. For example, Meera Bai, a popular royalty in the mediaeval Indian history. Sufi music is devoted in praise of the Lord. Different religions have varying concepts as regards the form of prayers or other religious practices. All these are perhaps in the domain of rituals, but their essence would largely be to transcend the illusion of this material world by realization of God.

Another form of love is familial love. Wikipedia has beautifully defined it as "a type of affinity or natural affection felt between members of a group bound by common ancestry or blood ties, or through friendship and care.[1]" This type of love is all encompassing. It begins at infancy and is directed towards parents. Later it expands to the siblings, and then to teachers and friends. This form of love provides the fundamental bonding

---

1. Familial love – Wikipedia, The free encyclopedia.htm

between immediate associations and is vital for sustenance and growth. Ideally, familial love is the one that is committed, selfless, emotionally full and reciprocated by the other.

Love for art is yet another form of love. People devote their life to learn and be creative artists, be it for music, dance, painting, literature, etc. This form of love transcends more towards passion. But devotion and selflessness are its vital components. I would place this form of love on a higher pedestal of selflessness because there is no individual who will respond. It is the yearning from within. The artist's heart and soul alone would decide whether his love or the mission has been accomplished. There are many creative artists who were considered mavericks during their lifetime and their work was recognized only after they were gone. In short, though their passion remained unfulfilled lifelong, this did not deter them for its pursuit.

Greek Love is yet another form of love. Though considered of modern origin, it can be traced back to pre-Christian era in Greece. Socrates and Plato have written amply on this form of relationship, which is a bonding between males of varying ages. Relationship between an adult male and an adolescent boy was considered a socially accepted form and perhaps in keeping with the responsibility the adult male shouldered to educate and train the boy in martial skills to excel in the mainstream. Amorous aspects may or may not have been the reason for this type of relationship. This gave rise to yet another term, Platonic Love, that is love between two individuals, where affections exist but intentions are chaste, sans any physical contact. This form of love has been glorified, as it is the main solace when either the love has not been requited or the union is impeded. The lovers still continue to fantasize about each other and be with each other in dreams and thoughts, if not in person.

Finally, love for oneself. It is a unique feeling where one is inspired by his/her own actions and perhaps success which sustains the motivation. This feeling could border on being egoistic or arrogant, though for a better cause. Creative minds, great leaders, social workers and great achievers with high self-esteem could fall in this category.

Modern science too has not left love alone. They have studied and tried to quantify this phenomenon, and have succeeded to a great extent. Massive strides have been taken in the field of biological science and neuroscience to unravel the mystery of the whys and hows of human response to love. Modern brain scanning techniques such as MRI are being used to explore which regions of brain are involved in the experiences and behaviours associated with love. Neuroscientists have discovered various neurochemicals triggered in the brain during various phases of love and their impact on human behaviour. To name a few, neurochemicals like dopamine, testosterone and oxytocin have been associated with sexual attraction and attachment, sexual behaviour and passion, and for long-term relationship respectively. A study by Laureen Slater in his cover page article '*Love; the Chemical Reaction*' of *National Geographic Magazine*, February 2006 issue has drawn a correlation between the neurochemicals and behaviour of the individual. He establishes that chemicals triggered are dependent on the nature of the activity and not on nature of the participating persons.

According to some bioscientists, love could easily be termed as an activity and not a feeling. Further, effort to externally regulate the levels of neurochemicals triggered would imply modifying the natural response of a person towards love. All this was having a deep effect on my perception of love. If subjected to brain mapping for study of my love quotient, one would feel as if being undressed in public. And if someone tried to modify natural behaviour for love, it would be catastrophic. Where would the purity of love go? What about the privacy, the feelings, the agony, the ecstasy, the attachment, sweet nothings, the romance? All innocence would be lost. I was not downplaying the role of science, but I felt ignorance would certainly be bliss for me in this case. I felt somewhat relieved that I had my answers to many of the persisting queries about love.

I felt that my original perceptions had withstood the research on love. In fact, these had only been strengthened in spite of the psychometric tools to quantify the feeling of love or to subvert its very existence and convert it into an activity. I maintain that love is divine. It is pure. It may have many forms, but the essence is a feeling of surrender and sacrifice. It is selfless. It does not seek reciprocity, though if reciprocity is there, it flourishes. Love of children for parents is reverence and gratitude, love for the divine is devotion, and love for the art or for any other thing or even profession could be passion. But all these are still love, true and pure. Love even in the ephemeral sense is for the beloved. This form of love is instinctive. It is natural. I feel it cannot be and should not be cultivated. It may or may not be at the first sight, but it is not deliberate. It does not weigh the pros and cons of any situation. One just falls in it, irrespective of the implications. It is not possessive. In fact, the best test of love is to allow it to drift away. If it comes back, it is yours; otherwise, it never was. Love is in the heart and not in mind. Love is mad. It does not see the flaws in the beloved. It does not see reason. It is the spring from where inspiration and courage to excel and outstand sprout. It is not necessary that everyone has to be in love. Respect, reverence, adjustment, and accommodation are accepted alternatives for many who have passion for other things, and also for those who consider love as frivolous or artificial. Love transcends all barriers, and is undeterred even if it does not culminate in marital bliss or communion. Therefore, it is the blessed that are destined to fall in love to experience this emotion even for a short while, or even if it is not requited. As Lord Tennyson said, "it is better to have loved and lost than never to have loved at all."

14

The Power of Touch

I know you are there somewhere;
how I wish thou to be besides me;
how I long for thy touch...

It was a murky day. Sky was overcast. Sun was hiding behind the clouds, light unable to penetrate beyond the nearest. Wind was imperceptible, weather torrid as if drooping with humidity. Environment was heavy and gloomy. Nature's freshness was visibly missing. It seemed as if nature had taken a day off. Sensing this, the happenings too had fallen in line. The day opened its account bereft of its freshness. Usual cheerfulness was nowhere on the scene. The smiles were absent. There was an air of withdrawal even in the interactions. Unpleasant news chose the day as if by design. Nothing happened as it normally did. All the forces spearheaded by nature seemed to have ganged up against me. I decided to call it a day. I stepped out and chose to take a walk; a walk down the solitary path leading to I didn't know where. I didn't seem to care. I found an isolated spot and settled down on a bench. Eyes blank, looking distant, but mind looking inwards, probing, thinking. What was happening? Why all this? Why me? No logical rationale was forthcoming. All this lasted for a while, till I felt a soft tap on my shoulder. It was her. She appeared from nowhere. Was it telepathy? She sat down next to me, took my hand and held it softly. No words were exchanged, nor was there any other communication. Her warm look and her presence felt through the touch said it all. All my stress melted away, and I soon broke into a smile. Restored, as if nothing had happened. I put it all behind me and got on with the day afresh.

Whatever may have been the cause and the effect, my turnaround was miraculous and was to leave a lasting impression on me. In reflection, I sensed that possibly nature had a plot. It had created a negative crescendo, taken it to abysmal depths, and then subtly turned it around to hope, making me, the victim, to first plunge to a depressive emotional state and then transcend to the other extreme; bordering on elation, merely by a simple stimulus of a touch. In all this, there was a subtle but powerful message: power of the touch. It was a revelation. This set me thinking. Many questions flashed. What exactly was this feeling of touch? What power it exudes to change the total perception of a person? Is it for real?

A touch is deemed to have taken place when the intervening space between two persons or even objects ceases to be, when their proximity is so close that physical contact takes place. This process may appear to be an ordinary physiological phenomenon, but has far-reaching impact on the psychological plane. Precisely from this moment onwards, the process of induction ceases to apply. Instead, the flow of electrons is triggered. In short, the sensation which till then was caused indirectly as induced perception by the electromotive forces now converts to direct and free flow of vibes, giving rise to the feeling, which comes by the perception of touch. It is a tender sensation; a sensation of warmth, of reassurance, of confidence, and of predictable response. This reduces stress and blood pressure and gives rise to a feeling of relaxation. This process of sensing a sense is made possible by the nervous system.

How does this entire nervous system work? Sensing a touch and converting it to a feeling with magical physical and psychological effects is an amazing phenomenon. Simply put, the information acquired by the sensory organs, eyes, ears, nose, tongue and skin, is transmitted to the brain, which in turn, processes it and transmits instructions back to the body for reaction. It appears simple but is a highly complex system.

Nervous system is triggered by the sensory organs which have specialized receptor cells. These cells act as out posts and transducers to gather intelligence and convert it into nerve signals, which are relayed to the brain by billions of tiny cells called sensory neurons. A complex electrochemical process makes it happen. Different parts of the brain swing into action to process these signals. The final destination of the incoming signals is the outer layer of the forebrain, the cerebrum. This layer is called the cerebral cortex, the gray matter. The information is processed here and decisions for reaction by the body are relayed through motor neurons. A small portion of these outgoing signals is also fed to other parts of the cerebrum; namely amygdala and thalamus, for storage in the memory and for a reflexive response in future to similar sensation. This neurological relay creates its paths which serve as the basis for memory and cuts down the response time. Sensory cells are unique for each sensation. In case of sensation of touch, these receptors are mostly concentrated in the fingers, tongue and the lips. Similarly, receptor cells for other senses are concentrated in their respective organs. Remaining parts of the brain and the Spinal Cord too play a vital role in all these neural transmissions. Entire process from end to end acts much faster in time.

If the peripheral description of the nervous system as discussed above is so complicated; one can but imagine the level of complexity in actual functioning of this system. It is astonishing as to how nature has thought of everything and created this wonderful and live network; a network which works round the clock, lifelong, unattended, unsupervised, precise, and balanced, involving meticulous coordination of intricate functions of so many parts of the body, brain and billions of cells. Surely this system is robust and may have inbuilt backups. It does not demand any specific external maintenance. But I am guarded to conjure a guess about the impact that even a minute impairment or malfunction of tiniest of the players in this neural chain may have on the response of the body. All this was getting much too complex. Wiser on the why and how of all this, I thought it best to put this load of back-end details on the back burner and revert to the aesthetic and psychological plane in the realm of the touch.

The feeling of touch is probably the ultimate of all the senses. All senses finally lead us to make a physical contact for better or worse. Although each of the senses is vital for our survival and living a complete life, the sensation of touch surely could be elevated to the exalted status of king of all the senses, should any comparison be drawn between these. The power of touch is not a new phenomenon. Most mothers have exercised this power intuitively on their offspring from times immemorial. Their petting, pecking and holding the child has always been a source of comfort and reassurance. Such children grow up well and normal. Their immune system is strengthened. They also grow up to be compassionate and caring adults. On the contrary, the children who have been deprived of the bliss of frequent and gentle touch of the mother, or of someone else taking care, feel psychologically deprived. They tend to hold it against the world and grow up to be aggressive and even violent in nature.

Touch is a human necessity; it sends out positive vibes which can have miraculous effects. A touch is not the need of the children alone. The adolescents require it for confidence and reassurance as they are ready to step out of the protective environment of their nests to seek new horizons, new experiences and new relationships including with the opposite sex. The adults require it because of numerous perceived or unperceived pressures generated by the challenges of life in work and in relationships. The old require it more than anyone else. It helps alleviate their perceptions of feeling of vulnerability to virtually everything, disease, loneliness, dependence on others, etc. A gentle touch is a stress buster; it releases tension, slows down the heart beat and reduces the blood pressure. It lifts the mood and one feels comforted. A male adult is too naïve to seek a touch, but surely needs one to diffuse stress. Women have soft skin and are naturally warm. A gentle and warm touch is a great stimulant for them and acts like an elixir. In short, a touch and its softness say it all. No amount of words can express this feeling.

There is yet another facet of touch, the healing touch. Many saints and god men are known to be endowed with healing powers in their touch. Jesus Christ cured a leper by his touch. The word spread about his miraculous powers and many more benefitted. Many ascetics are known to have acquired cosmic powers in their touch by meditation and penance. Although there is no scientific explanation for it, miracles are known to have occurred to people and continue to do so. We may brush these aside as a coincidence or a freak case. However, it will be naïve to discard this option totally because this may be the only hope left for a person suffering, and that too when the scientific alternatives have been exhausted and offer no hope. I believe it is a matter of faith. One has to believe in the need and in the power of the empowered one. If that be so, healing then is only a state of the mind; some relief is bound to take place. So why give up this option? It may well be the last straw.

Ultimate ecstasy of the feeling of touch lies perhaps in touching the person you love. In such case, the feeling is intense. One is ever yearning for a touch of his beloved. The touch arouses the feeling of love. The lovers are transported to their own world. Mere holding of hands, an embrace, a hug, mere brushing of their bodies and finally a kiss elevates them to a different plane. They are ecstatic in the caress, in blissful warmth of each other's presence. Nothing else matters to them. They are on cloud nine. Feeling of a kiss seals the issue. It is perhaps the pinnacle of the sensation of touch. Nature too has designed it to be so. It has subtly concentrated maximum sensory cells in lips and tongue.

Touch has a negative angle also, if it is intended to be so. It is the manner and pressure that decides the intent. A negative touch sends negative vibes. One senses these vibes fast. Defensive mechanism is activated, and one tends to react fast. Logic takes a backseat. Ironically, in many cases, incidences of a negative touch remain ingrained in the memory forever and reflect in one's psyche. Such cases could be parental bias, a teacher's admonishing, sibling rivalry, bullying classmates, dominating friends and the like. One has to be watchful of such tendencies in a person. Their response can be unpredictable.

There is yet another phenomenon associated with touch, touch-me-not. It pertains to typical defensive behaviour of some tropical plants and shrubbery which have weak stems. These are either prostrate or semi-erect. These have soft and sensitive leaves which fold and droop when touched. Similarly, there is yet another variety of Mediterranean vine which sheds its seeds and juice when touched. These phenomena will surely have a botanical explanation, but I can only conjecture that these plants and shrubs sense every touch as an intrusion. This term may generically be extended to some human beings also who, for some reason, are shy of human touch.

Wiser about the why and how of this wonderful gift of feeling of touch, I thought it only appropriate to reflect on my own experience of this feeling and its impact on my life. I was fortunate to grow up in an affectionate and caring familial environment. The social norms then existing did not encourage visible display of affections. However, I have fond memories of my mother's touch, which was always warm, protective and reassuring. I have had more than my share of positive vibes, though there was a mix of some negative ones too. The positive vibes have left a lasting impression on me. These have triggered compassion and empathy in me. I value the feeling generated by a warm touch and consider it vital for any relationship. A handshake conveys much more than a mere nod. It establishes a personal link. A hug and an embrace only intensify the sensation. Such a reach out comes naturally to me and has more or less become second nature with me.

I feel that the habit of communication by touch is vital not only for elders, but for children as well. A touch is expressive and its effect lasting. Pets, particularly dogs, are a great help in cultivating this feeling. Pets love to be fondled, to nestle and be snug with the master. It is a great sensation to feel their selfless love through their simple touch. Though keeping pets needs some effort and care, but there is plenty to learn from the pets. If children too come to love pets, they learn fast. They learn to respect values of life, bind closer as family and soon shed their inhibition to express their love by touch. I feel the effort involved in taking care of the pets is too small a price to pay for the payoffs. We have richly benefitted from this experience. The effect is visible even in the third generation. This may well nigh be our humble step in character building of the new generation; all this by the power of touch, be it of a human being or even of a pet.

Being sensitive to sensitivities of life, I am given to the charm of touch; to the charm of the feeling that it arouses and the power that a touch exudes. But the complicated neural process that makes it happen keeps flashing in the back of my mind. I shudder at the thought that a kiss is being observed by millions of neural observers sensing that information and billions of neurons acting as couriers jostling to inform the brain, and so many parts of the brain competing to compute this information against time to take a decision and speedily relaying it back to the lips for reaction. Funny, I thought! What reaction by the lips? To continue to kiss, to enjoy it or not, or what else? I wonder if even this act of kissing is on someone's orders, and if so whose? Who is controlling all this? I do not have an answer, nor do I want one. I think ignorance is a great bliss, and I will like to settle for that for now. I'd rather continue to relish the bliss; bliss of the power of the touch.

15

Are Memories a Baggage of the Past?

To die to the known is to have no continuity of yesterday.
That which has continuity is only memory...
-J Krishnamurti

Are memories a baggage of the past? Do we need to nurture them or shed them? Are they a source of inspiration or a hindrance to one's growth? Such thoughts have often crossed my mind. Finding no clear-cut answers, I kept these thoughts on the back burner and went along with life, sometimes drawing upon the memories and sometimes making efforts to shut them off my mind.

Much that I tried, I could not keep the lid on this topic for long. The thought was rekindled as I read a collection of discussions by the great philosopher J Krishnamurti in his compilation, *Commentaries on Living.* The discussions were about queries by some thinking minds seeking answers to various questions such as 'Is there a permanent state of love, of creativity, a permanent end of sorrow?' Krishnamurti analyses various aspects and states that "What has continuance, 'permanence', is the memory; memory of the things that have been. The mind must die to the past. The totality of the mind must be completely still, without any pressure, influence or movement from the past. Only then the other is possible".[1]

The questions that had been simmering in my mind surfaced afresh, seeking my response. The philosopher's analyses left me as confused as those seeking minds mentioned in the above discussions. While there is a tendency to think of the past and live in the future, to a traditional mind, the past has always been beautiful. One wants to cherish those memories irrespective of the fact that these may not have been really beautiful when the past was present. No doubt, the memories give a sense of continuity, an anchor, a source, a benchmark to fall back on. But in all these cases, the memories may not be memorable. Happy memories yes, but what about the miserable ones? Those too continue to haunt. Though memories do give a sense of permanence and continuity, these too may vary if filtered. One modifies the memories as the perceptions change, and these change regularly with time. Hence, these too are dynamic. What remains are dreams of correlation with happy memories or even tragic ones. One tends to brood and live in the past and lose sight of the present.

Are memories really a baggage of the past? It may not be possible to answer this in a single line. The answer could

---

1. Commentaries on Living, Third Series, by J Krishnamurti, pp 338-339; first published in India by Penguin Books, 2006.

be a simple yes or no. Certainly, previous influences tend to fetter one's thoughts. One is canalized to be a traditionalist or a conformist. The past controls the mind. Then how can fresh ideas germinate? The truth can continue to lie in wraps undiscovered. Obviously, this leads only to mediocrity. If one is content with this, he can formulate any amount of reasoning to justify his rationale. This is what distinguishes a creative mind from the rest.

A creative mind is focussed in its pursuit of truth. It yearns to be free, to soar unhindered. It is not scared of carving out a path of its own. It does not wish to be bonded or be a slave to a tradition, or a compulsive guide who may control his thoughts. It questions the fundamentals and the source itself. It does not recognize any boundaries. It invariably steps out to the uncharted territories. All this demands immense mental strength and moral courage. What could be his source of inspiration? His belief in himself and purity of his thought in search of truth inspires him. His focus provides the succor to generate the energy which becomes his strength. Oblivious to his personal comfort, he operates directly in the highest state of self-actualization. He is perhaps in a state of trance. He is like a light house which stands tall, though alone. He develops an aura radiating intrinsic energy which inspires many seeking minds to draw courage from his beacons. This path is arduous, success is not guaranteed, but is pure and inspiring. It needs courage and totality of mind to step out of the current domain and walk into the emptiness. Such personalities maybe less, but these are the people who shape the future of humanity. Should one not try to be creative in one's own humble way? This approach to life is as applicable in our day-to-day functions and interactions as it would be in research. If one is to remain tethered to previous knowledge and diktats of old memories, mediocrity may continue to prevail unless one is very strong willed. To that extent, memories are definitely a hindrance.

Surely memories do have a positive side too. Memories are the basis of our history. They make us relive our experiences. Experiences are what we gain from our failures. Therefore, to revisit these in our thoughts, though to recall the memories, may only help in drawing lessons for the future. Memories can also be a source of motivation for some. One may take up a challenge in life to do something in particular or to achieve something keeping in view the impressions of his past. There is yet another facet of memories; the human angle, the softer or emotional face. Memories of associations, memories of family, of romance, of love and of the dreams one dreamt of, of trauma, of tragedy, of abundance, and of deprivation. Any or all of these combined could be a source of strength or even weakness, depending on the attitude of a person. The positive effect is that one can go into a reverie and get recharged for the challenges ahead; the negative effect is that one could continue to brood and degenerate by remaining shackled to the past like descendants of old royalty.

Is it possible to retain the memories and yet remain unaffected by their negative influence? Ideally, one would like it to be so. Can one store all the memories, good or bad in a separate compartment of mind and switch it on or off at will? In that case, the urge to fall back upon fond remembrances need not be forsaken. After all, every passing moment becomes our past. In fact, our entire life before this very moment is our past. Is it fair to wipe out all this in one stroke just because some of these could stunt growth of the creative mind? Would this not be too harsh a cost? I feel it should be possible to have via media. It will depend on self-discipline or self-control. Therefore, the level will vary from one person to another, the idealist being at the top end of the continuum and the most sensitive one at the bottom. One could hold on to one's own memories and draw strength from them, or allow the mind to reflect and deliberately be swamped by memories of old associations, relationships, of one's unfulfilled desires, of what one missed in life and where one lost out.

Tragedy too has a charm of its own. That is why old songs are very popular. Only if one was mentally strong or sufficiently thick skinned to be immune to the negative signals from the past, it would be ideal to cherish the memories. These also guide us in assessing our own potential. One can then pitch at an accessible level in life and take one step at a time. This is bound to ward off uncalled for frustration and, therefore, lead to contentment and joy in life.

Level of creativity and mediocrity too is relative. It will be a direct function of mental resilience and ability of an individual to be independent of the past when it comes to his pursuits in life. Those who reach the epitome of creativity, say great scientists or thinkers continue to achieve unhindered, irrespective of their past and their memories. Their passion for their pursuit is not normal, it borders on even eccentricity. It is for us to decide what level one can pitch at and at which part of the spectrum of the continuum one may fit in. A few minds may shape the thought process but this planet still requires lesser cogs to run the system. Therefore, each one of us can contribute to the humanity in our own humble way. The bottom line is that one must learn to enjoy one's own pursuits and bring joy for everyone without allowing the memories to eclipse our behaviour.

Above thoughts removed the fog from my mind and demystified the queries simmering for such a long time. The answers crystallized. It helped me to take my decision towards my approach. Not surprisingly, I realized that I had been following this approach all along as a natural response. I have pursued my pursuits with an open mind on a clean slate with no complexes, complacency or hangover on account of the past. Although I have hung on to my past, I have tried to retain my sensitivities in my approach towards life. I do fall in some part of the continuum. I have amply contributed to the cause of the humanity and am continuing to do so in my humble way, and I am fairly content to be what I am with my memories intact.

16

On Loneliness

Pray that your loneliness may spur you into finding
Something to live for, great enough to die for...
-Dag Hammarskjold

As an observer of life, human behaviour has always intrigued me. My efforts to decode the charade only left me sinking deeper in this quagmire, groping for answers. Interestingly, every such attempt succeeded in raising yet more questions. Basic queries like why people behave the way they do, why no two persons respond similarly to the same situation, why do basic courtesies matter so much, why does one build an attitude, how does a creative mind create opportunities out of a situation considered hopeless by others, etc., continued to persist. The genesis of all this could perhaps lie in the psyche of each individual and his experiences which may have contributed to such a state.

A human mind is a bundle of complex emotions. These emotions could range from one extreme to another. These lead to the state of mind that one experiences, which, in turn, becomes the motive force behind one's behaviour. The state of mind could vary from being an extrovert, dominant, forceful, boisterous, playful, lively, and dynamic, to a temperate state of being considerate, amiable, accommodating, affectionate, and conservative and to the other extreme of being an introvert, recluse, self-centred, withdrawn and lonely. It was strange to learn that 'loneliness' is the dominant state in the total pie of human behaviour. Therefore, I realized that it was worth a deeper study. But what exactly is loneliness?

Loneliness is commonly understood as an emotional state of mind in which a person experiences a powerful feeling of emptiness and isolation. If that be true, then it is a dangerous state to be in. One needs to understand whether it is due to lack of physical or emotional contact with other human beings, or a feeling of wanting or of abandonment? Is it restricted to old age or the infirm? It was revealing to learn that feeling of loneliness stretched across the barriers of age, although old age does have a bearing. A person can be lonely even in a crowd, so it raises doubts on the basic perception that physical company may really not be the primary factor.

Next issue to consider is whether it is a state acquired by design or one has been forced into? This leads us to yet another phenomenon: solitude. Solitude is distinct from loneliness. It is a state when a person deliberately isolates himself to be a recluse to appreciate his time to reflect and use it creatively. Loneliness is generally considered a negative state, while solitude is a self-imposed state to avoid intrusion in one's privacy. Paul Tillich states, "Language has created the word 'loneliness' to express the pain of being alone, and the word 'solitude' to express the glory of the pain." Notwithstanding the semantics, both these states imply a state of being alone. Both cause pain and have often been used interchangeably.

I was amazed to find that so much has been written about loneliness. Interestingly, not everyone views it as a negative state. There is a happy blend of positive and negative perceptions regarding loneliness even among great thinkers. While Mark Twain described loneliness as, "be good and you will be lonely", Mother Teresa felt "loneliness and the feeling of being unwanted was the most terrible poverty". In short, loneliness encompasses both these facets; it is the way one perceives life. It could offer an opportunity to withdraw into oneself and blank out any intrusion and distractions. It would further create an atmosphere conducive to focus on one's own faculties and thoughts which may raise the plane to be one with your higher self. This is like a tonic to a creative mind. The mind soars and ideas flow.

All this sounds rather simple but is not easy to pursue even for a short duration, leave alone for sustained periods. It is a penance with no guarantees. One has to have a strong will, courage of conviction, determination, and purity of heart. But once initiated, the ball is set in motion. His attitude towards life changes, and he is at peace. He rises above the mundane. Material needs start losing meaning. He is in a state of bliss, in complete control of his mind, and can walk in and out of his self-created shell at will. Achieving such a state is a meditative journey for most, except perhaps for the born genius. The negative face could include a feeling of abandonment, longing for company, and a feeling of isolation and deprivation. This could only get worse if one is old, physically infirm, or financially in distress. Such people are highly sensitive in nature, generally pessimistic, and are not confident of their own potential. They carry the baggage of their past rather seriously, thereby perpetuating their misery. They feel vulnerable and widen the gap rather than build bridges with others. Thus, they tend to retract into their own shell and build a wall around themselves. They feel that they are by themselves and therefore are lonely. Their behaviour is a reflection of their psyche. They are the weaker minds who succumb to self-effacement and self-pity, choosing the easier path of avoiding the challenges rather than facing them headlong. Thus, loneliness becomes their destined fate. Their life becomes pathetic and miserable. Nothing good ever seems to happen to them.

I remember reading a short story, *The House of the Man Who has No One* by Nobel laureate Orhan Pamuk in his anthology, *Other Colours**. The author describes an isolated but once beautiful house atop a hill with a stunning view. It was owned by a man who lived alone. But it was not always that he had no one. He had a wife who was from far off and had no relations. Unfortunately, she fell sick and died. The man continued to live there in isolation. Since the view from the house was splendid and extraordinary, the author felt one could spend years gazing at the resplendent view of the hill, reflection of the sun in the sea, passing ships in the distance and so on. The author then observed that the house had been barricaded with large quantity of wires, cables and pipes. During a walk up the hill, when the author was outside his house, the man came out with an iron rod, gave a hard look and disappeared inside. The anecdote was so expressive of self-imposed isolation by the owner of the

* *Other Colours* by Orhan Pamuk, 1997. Translated from Turkish by Maureen Freely; first published in the UK by Faber and Faber, 2007, pp58-60.

house; he gave all indications of living in the misery of loneliness in spite of lavish splendour of nature around him. The author beautifully leaves a lot to the reader's imagination.

This story set me thinking. It was not an exceptional case; it could happen to anyone. Modern lifestyle only facilitates such a transition. It dawned on me that even we have settled down in a new place where we have no one and even our children are away. Such cases are aplenty, particularly in affluent societies and in big cities where everyone is so busy that they hardly have time for others.

It has become fashionable to meet the kith and kin at least once in a year. Ironically, in many cases, it remains restricted to that day only. It left me wondering if life is all doom and gloom, or is there a way out to sweeten it? While everyone cannot be a genius or a creative mind to relish being alone, one doesn't have to be at the extreme state of loneliness. Having to live alone at some stage of life is inevitable and should not come as a big surprise. Children have to grow up. They fly out to find their own vistas. The couple fashion their own routine and continue to nurture the nest. The birds return at their convenience. Unfortunately, modern day nuclear families have placed most of us in this unenviable state. If marriage lasts, husband and wife grow old together; they enjoy each other's company till death. Thereafter, one is alone. If one is single, one is alone all through. Therefore, the solution is not in finding a company or reassurance, but in learning to live by oneself. One has to learn to be alone and yet not be lonely.

To be alone is not such a complex state. One could be alone when even in company. There have been instances when even in a gathering one can retract to a compartment of his mind to enjoy his privacy. It was Pearl S Buck who said, "Inside me there is a place where I live alone and that's where you renew your springs that never dry up." Sometimes even friends can drain you. One seeks compatibility; in intellect, commonality of interests and in attitude towards life. Very often, it may become necessary to maintain a distance, albeit to be alone. A crowd is not a company and hence there is a need to be selective. As they say, 'it is lonely at the top'. If one has been catapulted to such an exalted position, then the leadership style may call for discretion in mingling with others. In all such situations, one can still convert this into an opportunity to pursue one's own passions. And if one does not have any passions, it helps to develop them. This could be the mantra for life and a panacea for loneliness.

I don't prophesize to be a psychologist or a soothsayer, but equipped with the above analyses, my mind became clearer. I understood that to enjoy being alone, one has to enjoy life and seek happiness and contentment. For this, one has to view life holistically and go back to the basics. I feel that one has to be simple, straightforward and transparent in inter-personal interactions, be humane and full of compassion, be honest in purpose and have the courage of conviction to seek and follow the truth. All this sounds too lofty and utopian or even moralistic, but we do learn these dictums as a child and follow them. Ironically, as one grows up, there is a tendency to drift away. Notwithstanding this, one can still revert to the purity and simplicity of childhood. If there is a will, then reverting to the basic tenets with a sincere and honest effort no longer remains utopian. Attitudinal change starts taking place. Although level of effort may vary from a person to person, once the plunge is taken, the transformation starts. One starts relishing life and savouring every moment of it. Loneliness disappears, and being alone is no longer a pain. I thought it best to apply the above hypotheses to myself and see how I was dealing with this challenge.

In reflection, I realized that all this was not mere rhetoric. I had been practising most of the above thoughts at a decent level. Maybe being a traditionalist had helped me. I cherished and sustained the values imbibed early in life. Although no bonanzas came my way, even minor successes inspired me. My will became stronger. At times, I thought that I did not get what I deserved, but the results started becoming less relevant gradually. Satisfaction and contentment came from within for having acted the way one felt was correct. Some thoughts and activities that influenced my mind and were catalytic to shape my life had been: *life is a precious gift, relish every moment of it; being positive is far more easy than being otherwise; one can never be alone in the company of the books; whenever anything untoward happens, one should thank God for small mercies as it could have been worse; one must develop some hobbies and pursue these with passion, these offer a purpose to life; feel rich as long you have sufficient for your basic needs, if not so then prune these needs; love, romance, music and art are for the fortunate ones, nurture these as they add flavour to life; and lastly, being physically fit is one's prime responsibility towards his body, pursue sports, yoga, etc., like a worship.*

At the cost of being immodest, I dare say that I have fared well to meet the challenge of loneliness or being alone. I have put the above mentioned theory and thoughts into practice. I am actually walking the talk. Deep into retirement, having lived a busy life, I have chosen not to pursue a second career, barring a short stint in the corporate world. My wife, a successful house maker is also simple, straightforward and content. We are not social birds but often take off to meet our children and our moorings to recharge our batteries. I am dabbling in my activities with the passion of a school boy. In fact, I am often accused of looking well below my years. Most people think I am very rich because I am liberal in my dealings with the financially poor. I don't hold back from a good cause. I follow a packed routine which includes taking care of my pet, practising yoga, golf, surfing the web, monitoring my investments and of my children, ample reading, squash and gym, TV and indulgence in some minor vices. Time is never enough. I am always late for the meals at the table. So whither the loneliness? As of now, short putts are a bigger challenge to me than being alone, if at all. But there is a catch. All is not so honky-dory after all. As long as the physical fitness lasts and the mental faculties are alert, the going is good. The moment God decides to remove His benign hand, my lifestyle may undergo a total change. I only hope and pray that my courage and will power will not fail me, and I will rally back to a modified routine and continue to talk about peace, happiness and contentment.

Incidentally, mine is not a unique model. If one looks around, there are many more which are better. No doubt the human mind is and will continue to remain complex. It will continue to be influenced by the events that impact one's psyche, fashion, attitude and guide the behaviour. But retaining one's control is still in one's own hands. Basic tenets of life are the backbone of human resilience. If one has the will, the values are intact and the fundamentals strong, then one can bounce back and continue to relish life and not be swamped by any untoward situations, loneliness notwithstanding.

17

The Final File

Let us not close our eyes to the ultimate reality of life.
Let us gracefully accept what cannot be changed...

On a fateful day, I got the sad news of demise of my dear colleague, popularly called VK. Our association went back to nearly five decades when we joined the National Defence Academy as cadets. We were young aspirants to be commissioned as officers in the Indian Army. We both had fairly successful careers. We chose different arms and thus drifted apart in our own streams. Thereafter, it was only a few times that some common career course, or posting to the same station, or a formation would bring us together. Over the years, our interests and growth varied. Although we were not thick pals, our friendship and camaraderie was a binding factor for our mutual respect. On the social front, the ladies too got along well. It was thus a pleasant coincidence that we both chose to settle down in the same station after retirement. This is where our long-tested association matured.

Unfortunately, this was also the time when VK fell prey to the horrendous disease of oral cancer. But he remained composed and displayed tremendous will power. He carried out a thorough research and went about the entire treatment systematically and with courage. Fortunately, the symptoms disappeared and the trouble appeared to be as good as gone. He reverted to his routine activities taking due precautions. Everything went on fine until this wretched problem resurfaced a few years later and with vengeance. This time again he did not lose his composure. He researched more about the disease and underwent the requisite and tedious treatments including radio emissions through implants, radio therapy, and finally surgery. All along he tried to lead a normal life showing no signs of despondency or surrender. However, the malignancy spread uncontrolled and after a bold but torturous last ditch stand, his body succumbed to it and thus was relieved of this trauma. The consoling thought was that he died a painless and peaceful death.

Although he maintained an intact front and conducted himself with dignity, it is not difficult to visualize the tremendous impact of such a suffering on him and his family. His wife, a silent supporter, was always in attendance. His doting sons were settled abroad and they constantly shuttled back home to take care of him.

In a way, we were thankful to God for having spared him and his family further misery. In such situations, the teachings of the *Bhagavad Gita* and their relevance become a revelation. One starts understanding the meaning of this body which is only an attire for the soul. The *Bhagavad Gita* talks of the permanence of the soul and not of the body, and the option for the soul to shed the tattered apparel of this body when the time comes. One starts focussing on detachment from material things, from achievements, from baggage of the past, from ego, from possessiveness, etc. One realizes the worthlessness of all the possessions and sensory pleasures. Need for peace of mind becomes all pervading. Although most of our teachings and literature reflect on the above stated philosophy of life, there is a tendency to turn a blind eye to it when we ourselves or our families are directly affected. Fortunately, in case of VK, his family was well aware of the unavoidable predicament. It was a question of when or how soon. So the transition to 'post-VK era' was not so unbearable. Next was the stage for resettling of the family and to recommence life sans VK.

This is where the final file became relevant. This file was an invention of my imagination. It was to be an aide-memoire for consolidation of assets and liabilities of the deceased, and entitlements of the legal heirs and in identification and implementation of the process for smooth inheritance. All this was to be done quickly and in a dignified and amicable manner, keeping the sensibilities of all concerned in mind. There was no standard format for this. I devised it as a kind of customized check sheet. Such a file assumes importance in case the husband dies first and the wife is not financially independent, the same as VK's case. Suddenly, from being a protected housewife, the lady is pushed to the forefront; forced to face the world and to handle all responsibilities, starting from the mundane day-to-day requirements to more complicated ones like management of property, finances, education, upbringing of the children and so on. Most vital of these is the financial management to meet all current liabilities and be balanced for the future.

VK and his wife had fulfilled their mandatory responsibilities, including marriage of their sons, well in time. They owned a residential property and had adequate savings. VK had been meticulous and had started preparing for the inevitable. At least one good thing about cancer is that it gives adequate warning. Therefore, there is enough preparatory time for smooth transition of assets.

I undertook the responsibility to facilitate rehabilitation of the lady, to settle important issues like pensionary and insurance benefits, transfer of title of the property, etc. Each such issue is simple and the process is well defined, yet the bureaucratic norms do not allow smooth transfer. Though appearing to be helpful, everyone wants to play safe. Instead of facilitating the process, they have devised long-winding formats and seek proofs even for the obvious. The affidavits are to be notarized and some have to be registered with the revenue authority. All this involves time, leading to delay in release of funds and additional expenditure. This also requires presence of the lady in person in various offices and court, and that too at an early stage of bereavement. All this is still required irrespective of the fact that she has already been declared the nominee, and a will is in place. I realized that knowledge of the Succession Act and the need for preparation and registration of the will is vital.

In short, it was tough on the lady. If this was so for an educated lady whose husband was of some standing, one can well imagine the plight of lesser informed and young widows with kids. And to top it all, if there is a dispute for inheritance, one could end up in a cesspool of legal battle. True to my promise to VK of my being available for any thing, any time, anywhere, I went about the rehabilitation issues with a great sense of urgency. That would be one way of restoring confidence of the lady to face the challenges in store and reducing her agony to an extent. All the issues were attended to promptly and brought to logical conclusion. In doing so, I realized that I needed to organize my affairs too. Hence, I commenced work on my own file. This challenge had suddenly thrown up an opportunity. Being fresh from VK's case, I started preparing my own final file with great vigour and enthusiasm. However, with time, the enthusiasm started ebbing and the issue started taking a backseat. I suppose complacency had started setting in.

My determination to continue with the preparation of my own file did not last long. A strange thought crossed my mind when reflecting on the recent happenings. I felt it comic to be so enthusiastic and in a feverish hurry to prepare for my own end and that too so systematically. As if it will take away the charm of that event. Surely, there will be some well-wisher like me in my case too, who will take charge of the incomplete file. My mind also justified my lethargy again by the fact that the ladies too had got talking to each other on these issues, so were better informed. So I put the project on hold for the time being with lesser guilt. Soon I reverted to my routine with an increased vigour as if nothing had happened and nothing was going to happen, ironically contradicting my own observation earlier on the ultimate reality of life. What am I waiting for? Another trigger?

18

On Golf Practice

Golf is an amalgam of concentration and perfect harmony between the mind and body...

Golf is a sport with a difference. Once a person is initiated to it, it ceases to be a mere sport. It becomes a way of life. A golfer thereafter talks golf, eats golf, drinks golf and even dreams of golf. Unlike other sports, its handicap system acts as an in-built counter to the level of play and the aging effect as age has a definite bearing on the handicap. In a handicap tournament or a game, a higher handicap player has a fair chance to compete with a better player, who will have a lower handicap as his net score would be leveled by deducting his handicap from his gross score. Same applies to the lower handicap player. Thus, in reality, one is playing against his own handicap. Invariably most of the club level tournaments are held as handicap tournaments, and same is the case for even a friendly game. This keeps the interest of competition alive for all levels of players. No wonder it is not uncommon to hear about active golfers in the 80s and 90s.

So, what is so special about golf? First, golf is perhaps the toughest sport to master. It demands a perfect blend and devotion of the mind and body. All this has to be applied in rhythm, perfect harmony and coordination, scientifically and artistically. A multitude of muscles and nervous networks come into play in planning and execution of a single shot. The entire process of a golf stroke is symbolically akin to playing a musical instrument and producing a perfect note. Even a slight mismatch will produce atrocious results like jarring music in a discordant orchestra. Further, one does not need to create external challenges as a source of inspiration to perform. The standards for every course is well defined and one is pitted against the course and his own potential.

Golf is considered to be a gentleman's game. You can play competitively even by yourself, self-imposing the penalties as applicable, though referees are available to help in a tournament. Golf helps build self-discipline, mental tenacity and perseverance. One feels motivated to strive for perfection. In short, it helps strengthen the character qualities and values. It can become a source of inspiration to excel. Notwithstanding the result of a competition, beating one's own score or even a well-executed shot has a charm of its own. One long drive, one long putt, one chip in, one good recovery shot out of the woods can give an unmatched thrill.

No other sport provides such a true measure of self-assessment of one's performance and potential as golf. One learns the need to be focussed and inculcates immense power of concentration. It is a great stress buster. Golf too generates its own stress, but it is of a different nature. It encourages competition and makes the adrenaline flow. I would rather call it a meaningful stress; a stress that enables a player to focus and produce his best. This stress takes over and relieves the player of any other tension that he may have been subjected to. Of the two, this form of stress would be preferred any day. It will be incorrect to assume that everything is perfect about golf. It has its share of negative attributes. It is for an individual to understand and balance the pros and cons.

It is a myth that golf facilitates furtherance for the ambitious, as it provides an opportunity to rub shoulders with the high and mighty. Some believe this sport is for the social climbers as it helps a back-door entry to the socialites, or for corporate clan to clinch the issues. On the contrary, it might turn out to be just the opposite. Golf is a double-edged weapon. In an exuberance to make a quick impact, playing golf with those who matter, one may only make a quick and unnecessary exposure of his negative traits, which otherwise could remain under the wraps. In short, it does not afford any shortcuts to life. One has to work hard to derive the pleasure that one is looking for. It is vital to understand this aspect if one is picking up golf with the above-stated views in mind.

It is not uncommon to observe golf as an obsession with quite a few. Many golfers tend to spend too much time on it. All this comes at a cost. Cost of time and effort for other commitments. Invariably, the family is the most affected party. One may have heard of a strange term, 'golf widow', coined for such golfers' wives. Therefore, there is a need for time management with all golfers. As regards the time and effort for golf, every golfer has an urge to attain perfection and improve his score. Depending on the time and resources at hand, the effort gets translated into costs for procurement of latest equipment, enhanced frequency of the game and perhaps a set of lessons thrown in. At the end of all this, one finally reaches his level of competence. The reality then dawns that any further improvement will require a revolutionary change in the basic game under supervision of a professional coach. This would invariably involve unlearning what is already known and relearning afresh. This is a tedious process and demands massive effort and is a hard decision. Should one take the plunge of the pro route at this stage, it is quite possible that one may be left confused between the revised and his old swing. The mediocre mostly settle for the status quo. Thereafter, it is a smooth sail. They restrict their practice sessions to be able to stay in the existing groove and maintain their established level. Such players may be mediocre in their game, yet are ardent in spirit. Notwithstanding all this, all is not doom and gloom for this category of golfers, which incidentally forms the bulk of club level golfers. They are content with their game and continue to enjoy playing against their handicap.

It is interesting to observe a phenomenal level of game amongst the young crop of players, who have been initiated through professional coaching. Their effortless long drives with woods, scientifically executed shots with irons for mid-level distances, accurate pitch shots attacking the pin with a wedge, precise chips rolling next to the pin and consistent putts put many of us to shame. This only emphasizes on the need to start the game young, preferably under a coach. Even if someone begins late in life, it should be under a professional. Notwithstanding all the hurdles and expenses, the bug of golf once bitten continues to tickle the minds of one and all.

Applying all the above to myself, I assessed my game pragmatically. Although I have had quite a few successes under my belt during my long golfing career, I realized that the standard had remained of club level. There was consistency, with occasional flashes, with many wins but restricted to only handicap tournaments. Having been initiated into golf by self-learning, thanks to my agility and natural aptitude, my game reached a fairly dignified level fast and was bolstered by many club-level wins. Thereafter, for any substantial improvement, I had to go through the same process, that is, of total unwinding and then rewinding under a coach. I did make a sincere effort, but found it rather hard to attempt this change so late in life. I chose to revert to my original game opting for the famous status quo.

However, feeling the need to manage my time better, keep my family commitments in view and to pack many activities in a day without compromising on golf, I devised an innovative routine for myself. I decided to restrict the rounds of golf and replace some of these with focussed practice sessions. This approach is not novel. The pros practice regularly. In their case, it is their profession. However, most amateur golfers revert to the range only to correct their game, or experiment with some shots, or try out new clubs. The amateurs normally abhor going to the range unless it is absolutely necessary. In my case, it was a decision to be out, to enjoy golf, play as many shots and yet compress the time. The underlying motive was neither to spend too much time, nor to tire too much and yet continue to get the feel of golf. All that I had to contend with was to keep the devil of monotony from setting in. For this, I had to devise many variations during the practice sessions.

On a practice day, I would be more relaxed with adequate time for my pre-golf activities. There would be no rush to meet the deadlines of tee times, of a game fixed, etc. I would venture out to the course at will, even around noon in spite of the heat and wind conditions which many others may not be comfortable with. One obviously has to be motivated for all this. Who else would be? Who else would be out at that time braving the heat and the windy conditions all by himself? I also felt it to be advantageous to practice in these trying conditions. Playing the round in cooler conditions would be much easier. Therefore, I am inspired to shoot on the range.

Even at this odd hour, I am not alone. I have my friends with me. The balls, clubs, who do the talking, and the caddy, who also doubles up for a company and a critic of sorts. I have a perfect equation with them. I am focussed, concentrating on every shot, playing virtually all the clubs, communicating with the ball through the medium of strokes. It is a pleasure to see the ball lift to the desired loft and reach the intended distance dropping next to the target point. This goes on and on with the variety of the clubs. One is in perfect harmony with the nature and the shots, totally oblivious of the ambience. It is a pleasure to see how a minor change in the stance, grip, back swing or follow-through changes the profile of the shot. It is like a meditative experience. All that I try and practice for is to achieve consistency of distance and loft with any specific club, irrespective of the fact that a pro or a younger player may hit the same distance with a much lower club. I ignore it since I have no choice as I chose to maintain the status quo. But I do so without any feeling of guilt or shame for the number of years that I have put in and yet being outdriven by children. Although on a good day, I do give them a run for their money. It is also a matter of solace, if at all, that there is a yet better golfer even amongst the professionals. They also fret. Senior pros are being outdriven and outplayed by much younger pros. So I have no reason to feel otherwise. It is all relative, as it is in life. All this is still heavenly. And at what cost? Nominal. Time consumed: less than half of that for a round. External irritants: nil. Pay offs: tremendous. A good practice session makes my day. A bad practice session in any case is a better option than a bad round. I cut down so much from my otherwise potentially a bad time.

19

On Arthritis

My message is: keep moving. If you do,
You'll keep arthritis at bay.
-Donna Mills

Arthritis. What an unearthly name! The very thought conjures agony and mental trauma, not to forget the physical pain. So common, so visible and affecting so many. Every other person in his late 50s is susceptible to this or to one of its many forms. All forms of arthritis offer pain. The pattern of pain may vary depending upon the type and the affected organ or joint, but pain will be constant and unbearable. It is not uncommon to see many senior citizens with a limp. The disability thus caused affects the mobility of an individual, forcing him to modify his lifestyle. Should the individual happen to be an outdoor type, the impact can be disastrous. Could one keep this wretched affliction at bay? Only if wishes were horses! It is perhaps one of the most rampant and visible diseases. Though mostly age related, it does not leave even the young alone, be it under the garb of genetic disorder or on pretext of heredity. Poor elders, turning in their graves, being blamed ex parte for perpetrating this as their legacy; helpless and unable to contest in posterity. I too had a brush with this unfriendly phenomenon and have tasted fair amount of agony. Hence these reflections.

What exactly is arthritis? Arthritis derives its name from the Greek word 'arthro', meaning joint, and 'itis', meaning inflammation. Arthritis is a group of conditions involving damage to the joints of the body. It is the leading cause of disability in people older than 55 years.[1] Arthritis is of different types, most common ones being osteoarthritis and rheumatoid arthritis. The former owes its origin to degradation of the cartilage due to wear and tear, and aging. Cartilage is the fluid which provides cushion and lubrication between the articulate bones of the joint. Degeneration of this fluid causes direct friction of the bones resulting in excruciating and grinding pain. The pain becomes intense with movement, hence rest helps. This manifests predominantly in major load-bearing joints like knees. The latter (rheumatoid arthritis) is caused due to inflammation or swelling of the membrane that lines the joints. This also leads to destruction of the cartilage, causing stiffness and swelling of the joints. The stiffness so caused eases with exercise. This disability, superimposed by the associated medicines for its treatment, can also trigger degenerative process affecting various vital organs like heart, lungs, kidneys, eyes, etc. Being inflammatory in nature, this form can occur at any age.

---

1. Wikipedia, The Free Encyclopedia, http://en.wikipedia.org/wiki. Arthiritis

There are many other forms of arthritis which are more specific and more complicated. Lesser one knows about these the better. Ironically, in spite of falling in the susceptible age, and actively exercising, I was totally ignorant about this disease, its causes, symptoms, and precautions. My presumptions were contrary to medical thought. But these had worked till then. Would I have changed my lifestyle or curtailed my outdoor life on mere preventive advice, I am not sure. All this went on till it actually happened and I had to face it headlong.

First indicator came when I experienced an innocuous pulsating pain in my left knee during a mild climb in the golf course. It came and disappeared. A few days later followed yet another surge. Thereafter it was regular and constant all along, painful yet bearable. Bravado or whatever, I ignored it, hoping this to be a passing cloud. The pain not only persisted but became more intense. Was it there for keeps? I had no answers.

I had a passion for yoga, golf, squash, gym, and other outdoors all along and had pursued these to the extent possible through out my career of nearly four decades in the army. Being physically fit, I had continued to lead similar, if not more intense a life style even after retirement. My daily routine was packed and was a blend of my out door and intellectual pursuits. Sports had kept my body fit and my mind fresh. Being fairly good at these, I was more in contact with the young; this kept me youthful. This had been my way of life, and was continuing to be so, interestingly even at a faster pace, now that I had more time at hand. I could not think of a life different from this.

Although I could continue with my games, while walking or playing golf, I felt acute grinding pain in the knee joint at some angles. Playing squash, which too had continued unabated, which involves stretching in spurts, sudden change of direction and shifting of body weight, I found my movements in some directions seriously hampered. But I learnt fast. I modified my game so as to control the play to be more on my right side, load bearing capability of my right knee still being intact. I would apply a balm and play on. Ironically, I was still continuing to play well and enjoying. Little did I realize the metabolic changes that had adversely affected my knee joint and further aggravation that I was causing by continuing at the same pace? Maybe my ignorance, ego, pride, fear of disturbing my routine, or image of being super fit beating the age came in my way. I was hoping that my standard mantra of sweating it out when in an ailment, would work in this case also. Alas, it was not to be. I could not even visualize any different style of life as an alternative. So I continued, limping my way through, with dignity, though in great agony, never showing it on my face, trying to make it the least perceptible to others, stretching my will power to the edge. All this finally came to a dead end one day, when someone pointed out about my limp, and observed that the aging process perhaps may have caught up. This pained me more than the physical pain. That was the moment. The moment of truth. The truth that I had been trying to close my eyes to. The truth that I had to face.

My visit to the orthopedic surgeon was not too encouraging. An x-ray, a few usual questions, and prompt came the diagnosis. My age and family history, all my elders had or were suffering from arthritis, sealed the issue. The verdict: I was a case of osteoarthritis, the onset of which had only been delayed, if at all, thanks to my active life style. To reduce the severity of pain, I was advised rest, and physiotherapy of a variety to include laser, short wave diathermy, interference therapy and what not and finally wax bath. To my dismay, I was to learn that the damage caused to my cartilage was irreversible, and that there was no cure for this. I had to learn to live with this. Hot and cold packs, specified exercises including swimming could help though temporarily. Aids and supports like knee braces, walking stick, walker, maybe graduation to wheel chair were all a possibility in time. Short term remedy; painkillers, with attendant side effects, cortisone injections in the knee cap in an emergency, and finally surgery, arthroplasty or total joint replacement. All this was happening too fast. I was hardly able to absorb. In one single stroke, my life was being put in total disarray. My world was crumbling. I had to decide. I took the hard decision. I chose to continue with my life style, albeit out doors with a blend of intellectual activities, pain or no pain. Simultaneously, I also decided to stem this rot and eradicate it if possible, my own way. I decided to go all the way to evict this unwarranted intrusion in my life.

After some research for alternate therapies and with the support of my family, I opened multiple fronts against this enemy. Yoga was the foremost, fortunately I had been practising this for years, all that I did was to integrate some specific poses and *asnas* for strengthening the knee muscles with my regular yoga. In addition, I started exercising to strengthen the quadriceps and hamstring muscles of the leg initially on the equipment and later modified them so as to pursue them at home. These would eventually help release the pressure on the degenerated cartilage. Laser and interference therapies continued for a while, but I found wax bath to be more effective. Wax bath requires a thermo-controlled bath and involves dipping the affected joint in molten wax; thereafter insulating the solidified layer, enabling the latent heat so generated to penetrate deep within to the damaged tissues. This is a painful process, but very effective. To save time of visits to the hospital, we created simplified facility for wax bath at home. I also tried out alternate hot and cold pack therapy. Pain soothing balms formed a part of my sports gear. Application of these prior to and even during the game helped numb or distract the pain for a while. I shunned intake of any painkillers.

All these efforts continued along with my sports, my intellectual pursuits, family routine, social circle, etc., at virtually the same pace as earlier. I could feel some progress. The pain persisted but was less excruciating. This grueling routine stretched for a few months. The problem had probably been arrested, but the damage already caused had yet to be restored. Finally, we chanced upon a food supplement, a commercial combo of glucosamine and some proteins, in a health magazine. My sister, who was also my co-sufferer, and co-inheritor of this common loss, had tried it. This clinched the issue. I found a miraculous relief. In a matter of a few days the pain was as good as gone. In fact I bounced back with vengeance, stronger and fitter. Fortunately, I am continuing to be so even more than five years hence. Physiotherapy and wax bath were put on a hold, although the wax bath kit is always at hand. The integrated exercises in yoga have continued, the food supplement is continuing but on a much lesser dosage and frequency. I feel, I am free from the wretched disease. Maybe the cartilage tissues have been auto repaired or the supporting leg muscles, the quadriceps and the hamstring have become fairly strong to make up for the persisting damage, if any. I do not want to know more about this.

In reflection, I cannot confidently place my finger on any one single factor which may have been the cause to eradicate above ailment. I feel it must have been the result of combined effect of the holistic effort. Maybe I was in the initial stages of the disease, but I was not given much hope or assurance. Besides blessings of the divine, I view it is the will power, faith in own actions and unstinted support of my family which have helped this miraculous reversion of the irreversible. I have no intentions of challenging the theory, nor proselytizing as the know all on this. But I can only suggest that we should accept such verdicts only with a pinch of salt. All theories, including medical diagnosis have an element of probability. When the probability of occurrence of a disease for certain symptoms is say 99%, for the remaining 1%, probability of occurrence is zero. You maybe in that 1%. So rather establish that first before succumbing to the obvious. In all humility I have dared to share my experience, and cannot help but endorse the old adage that, where there is a will, there is a way.

20

On Reading

If we encounter a man of rare intellect,
We should ask him what books he reads.
-Ralph W Emerson

It was a beautiful day. The ambience was scenic. The clouds were playing hide and seek with the sun. The breeze was mild, brushing past, leaving a simmering tinge in the spine. Lush green valley was inviting. Intoxicating fragrance of the wild daffodils filled the air. Pine trees lining the valley were swaying in reverence. There was a trail of pretty maidens in the distance who were gathering mushrooms and singing the folklore. It was an ideal setting; ideal to step out, to take deep lungful of the rich abundance of the nature and savour every moment of it. I was mesmerized, praying if time could stand still so that I could capture this moment for ever.

All the above reminded me of the settings in writings of my favourite authors whose writings have held me in awe, whom I revere for their repertoire, though not necessarily agreeing with their views. It is their thoughts, their energy, their conviction, their empathy, and most of all, their ability to absorb the ambience and relate it with such beauty that transports the reader to the thralldom of their fantasy.

Sitting in the verandah, viewing the grandeur of nature, a book in my hand and sipping hot tea, I was transported decades back in time when I was initiated into the bliss of reading; reading beyond the casual glancing over the news and the glossies, but into the realm of reading with a purpose. I vividly recall a plethora of questions that churned in my mind. Reason: I was a student of science pursuing my formal studies, heading for a profession and some sports. One could visualize, the time that one had to take out for this new venture, if at all. Hence this debate with myself for diversion of my time and effort into the field of literature. Interestingly, whatever I had considered in my mind then holds true even today. Nothing has really changed except that a new dimension has been added to the writings, courtesy the web. As a result, a fresh breed of authors has mushroomed, the bloggers. Now, anyone can express their views freely on any topic. This only widens the scope of reading.

So what good is this famous activity of reading? Is it worth investing in? And if so, to what extent? Does one gain information, knowledge, mere narrative, or only a point of view which too may be biased? Is it a creative activity? Should it remain an activity, or become a habit, or even a way of life? What may be the ideal stage in life to take this plunge? How should one select what to read? And finally, what may be the impact of reading on one's life? In short, all these and many more queries may arise before one decides to take a serious plunge in the unfathomable depths of the written word.

Reading is a shortcut to access the lofty heights of research, observations, analyses, and finally knowledge of a writer's lifetime of hard work. All this is available on a platter and for the asking. Socrates averred more than four centuries before Christ, "Employ your time in improving yourself by the other man's writings; so that you shall come easily by what others have laboured hard for." Reading, therefore, is a ladder for self-improvement; an exposure to the vision of the visionary. In doing so, one makes a friend; a friend in a book for life, a friend who is reliable and never betrays you. Books communicate with you, enlighten you, and fill your time creatively. Omar Khayyam immortalized the companionship of a book in his famous quatrain, "A book of verses under the bough; a loaf of bread, a jug of wine besides me thou; Singing in the wilderness Oh; The wilderness would be a paradise enow."[1]

The fruits of the tree of wisdom are there to pick through the route of reading. Therefore, the earlier one starts this journey, the better. Fortunate are those who take up to literary pursuits early in life. But it is not all that easy. Parents, friends and teachers play a vital role in creating the right environment and expose the young minds to the world of books. However, they can at best lead him to the edge. Courage and motivation to step forward to imbibe reading as a habit and to draw inspiration to sustain it has to come from within. The liking to graduate from comics to a

1. *Rubaiyat of Omar Khayyam*, AD 1048–1123

book and sustain the interest has to be intrinsic. This initial phase of breaking in is perhaps the most difficult. It is like planting a tree. Once the seed is sown, it germinates into a seedling, and the sapling sprouts. The sapling being tender needs careful handling, nutrients, incentives, and some diversions. Soon the roots firm in. Thereafter, the plant is self-sustaining and the urge for reading flourishes unhindered. One soon gets sucked into the vortex and is, as if, transported to a different world; a world in which one can go on exploring the wealth of knowledge that lies hidden between the covers waiting to be dusted off and devoured. As one goes along, one also gets to learn more and more, as to how much more is there to learn. In this long journey of self-discovery, time is ever falling short. Early birds, no doubt, get a head start. They go past the light fiction stage in a stride and develop their personality early to channelize their reading. No wonder most intellectual minds have invariably taken to reading early in life. However, this should not deter others. Realm of reading is like a universal faith which welcomes anyone willing, at any stage of life, without any discrimination whatsoever. Therefore, it is never too late to take the plunge. Once on board, one has to make a choice of what to read.

Selection of reading is the biggest dilemma, for there is so much to read and so many fields to cover. In an anxiety to cover everything, one may end up disillusioned. Adolf Hitler, who was a voracious reader, in his work, *Mein Kampf*, stresses on the need to be selective in reading. Many factors may impinge on selection of reading. First, what may be the aim of taking up this activity? Should it be restricted to one's profession, or expanded to the field of interest chosen for study? Should it be fiction, non-fiction, biography, thriller, romance, history, philosophy, classics, semi-classics, religion, mythology, or informative? All these vary with the individual, his interest, his need, his level of comprehension, his ability to sustain interest, and finally the time available. One has to channelize the reading and start at one end. While most readers may start initially to fill their time creatively; some graduate to serious reading with passage of time. At some stage in life, they still have to make a choice to channelize their reading.

Reading and thinking are two sides of the same coin. Mere reading without reflecting or thinking is like skimming the surface of the iceberg. Real depth of knowledge is revealed only once the mind is applied. Thinking digests whatever has been read and converts it into knowledge. Reading is not a race to cover maximum stretch against time. It absorbs the material and provides nourishment for enrichment of the soul. It provides food for thought. One starts relishing this bliss. This reinforces the importance of selection of reading. Selection of a book is like choosing a companion. A companion who will be with you for a while and whose impressions may continue to linger even after it has parted. Everyone selects his own mix and blends the variety like a connoisseur to suit his temperament and desire. Selection of the type of reading, the theme, topic, author, book, single book or multiple books going at the same time etc., are typical for each reader.

Reading is not an exercise of mind in isolation. One reads, reflects, digests, absorbs, retains some and rejects the rest. He is experiencing the world of the author, who transports him to his realm. The reader shares the thoughts and rationale of the author.

Whatever be the level and content of the book, there will always be something to pick up. If nothing else, it is an experience. Even a negative experience is an experience. The experience enervates the reader's mind. With time, the learning process takes roots. He gravitates to higher levels of intellect. His mind soars to lofty heights in pursuit of information and knowledge. It is this process which transforms him. Knowledge induces subtle changes in him. It induces humility, positive vibes in attitude, compassion and empathy. He rises above the mundane. His material needs reduce gradually. His yearning for intellectual needs intensifies. He is at peace with himself and is engrossed in the bliss of his world of reading. He needs no company to fill his time. His mind is ever inquisitive. He observes and learns and his awareness increases. He can understand others' problems better, and becomes more tolerant and empathic. In short, reading has a holistic impact on the reader, on his mind, his body and his behaviour, which in turn impacts his life and lifestyle. Equipped with all these observations and analyses, I reverted to reflections down the memory lane, digging into my subconscious mind as to where did I figure in this literary conundrum, and how had this impacted me down the years?

I was a late starter for obvious reasons. In my early years, the environment was hardly conducive. Reading anything other than own texts or related material was considered frivolous. Only saving grace was that during vacations, I could take the liberty of reading some fiction, some good classics or semis sharing with my elder siblings. I fondly read works of famous authors like Tagore, Sarat Chandra Chattopadhya, and even translations of Gorky. Tagore's *Gora* gave an insight into the Bengali society in the colonial backdrop of the Raj and the renaissance movements to liberalize the harsh rituals and malaise of orthodoxy of the then Hindu society. Chattopadhya's works like *Biraj Bahu, Devdas* and *Shrikant* were very absorbing. He focussed on Bengali rural society and wrote against superstitious beliefs and oppression against the women.

I vividly recall the parting advice of my guide on the eve of my commission as an officer in the Indian Army: "An officer is always in the show window. Never appear to be doing nothing, even if you have nothing to do. Always keep a book at hand." This advice found its mark in me. Instead of mere façade or an escapade for a compulsive requirement, reading grew on me. I became fond of it, and soon it became a way of life with me. The first book that I bought was *Jude the Obscure* by Thomas Hardy. Hardy's command of language, his penetrative power of observation, his piercing eye for detail, his vivid description of nature, intense emotional sensitivity of his characters and absorbing flow of his expression kept me spellbound. His ability to infuse life into the characters transported me into his world; one could feel as if Hardy was narrating from his own life or experiences, perceptively in the first person. In spite of a strong lobby of critics, his writing on themes like live-in relationship, considered bold in the then contemporary society, speaks of his courage and conviction. Later, I read many of his other works as well. Out of these, *Tess of the d'Urbervilles* impressed me the most. His writings were reflective of power of truthfulness and conviction.

With time, the dilemma of selection of reading caught up with me too. Being in the profession of arms, I had to fine tune my reading. I felt that there was a need for professional reading besides the national and global current affairs. I wanted to cover the maximum in the little time that I could find. I devised an innovative method for myself. I diversified my reading by taking up a number of books on a variety of subjects, all at the same time. I would progress on all of these on a regular basis and finish one set. Then spend time again for the next pick. I have deliberately avoided picking up speed reading. I am reading for the love of it, and wish to absorb at my own pace. My reading is relatively slow, but deliberate and therefore very selective. This has been my way all along and is still so after I have shed my uniform. However, I have plenty of time for myself now and am in a position to pursue my literary pursuits with greater fervour and intensity. After I got this bonanza of time, I realized what all I have missed in life. I had hardly read Shakespeare, barring a book here and there. I was all the time interested in our scriptures, the *Vedas*, the *Upanishadas*, the *Puranas*, but hardly had gone past the great epics of *Mahabharata* and *Ramayana*. I had read the *Bhagavad Gita* but it was only translation. I needed to learn *Sanskrit* to read these works in original. I loved history, but had hardly read much except some isolated works here and there. There was so much to read about life in writings of Plato, Socrates and many more.

Notwithstanding the above, I draw inspiration to catch up on all that I have missed. I am approaching on multiple fronts simultaneously and systematically. I regret that I did not make any serious effort to learn Sanskrit. I have read the translations of many scriptures, but yearn to read the originals. In the interregnum, I am always looking for better translations. On the remaining subjects, I am progressing well. Though the pace is brisk, yet there is so much to read. As the natural follow up, this habit has triggered in me an urge to pen my thoughts and experiences. The urge is now well past the embryonic stage. It is already ticking. I hope to get somewhere sometime soon. I am resisting the temptation to venture into the new vistas of the blogosphere; I wonder how long I can hold on. Time is always falling short.

I do not claim to be a littérateur, but I dare say that I am creatively busy. I do have fair amount of diversions of outdoor activities interwoven in my daily routine. This keeps the adrenaline flowing and helps keep my mind fresh. It gives me the energy to stretch myself to the limit. Time is passing fast and well. That says it all for the impact of reading on my life and style of life. Reading has been and continues to be blissful for me. I am grateful to my guide for his wonderful piece of advice. In all humility, the only legacy that I will like to leave is this bliss of reading as a habit.

Section-III
Life As I See It

21

It Seems Like Yesterday

Firm roots anchor growth. Growth is the soul of life and life is the perpetuation of legacy…

It seems like yesterday. I was sitting on a chair besides my father, watching and trying to fathom him and his personality. He was a mid-level government officer, a man of modest means with adequate family liabilities to boast of. A responsible family man, he was an enigma, a mysterious personality, very private, never sharing his moments of glory or pressures, very focussed, very hard crust, very conscientious, very accurate, highly principled, very demanding from his subordinates and himself, always busy with his work, rarely interfering, never inquiring, almost giving an impression of being too self-centred, and perhaps casually interested in his wards. He was invariably meticulously dressed in good British attire, with a hat, his hallmark. He had a large social circle of friends and was a popular host, but from us, his children, he maintained some inexplicable distance verging on formality. He was rarely expressive of affections or concern so to say. Secretly, I disagreed with this model of parenthood. Notwithstanding this, the family affairs went on smoothly. There was seldom any money talk within the family, and we grew up normally, excelling in education and later in profession. One took life in its stride, never questioning, and always enjoying what one got.

My father retired in due course, having discharged his professional and family responsibilities. At this stage, he undertook a philanthropic cause to take care of the poor and needy children of the society. He created an organization that looked after the needs of such children. He devoted his full time free of cost, even chipping in some out of his modest resources to bring up these children under personalized care from infancy till they became self-sufficient and were rehabilitated in the society.

His personality flourished with time. He developed an aura of deep satisfaction and contentment. His face always glowed. We watched senior serving dignitaries visiting his humble abode for their own peace of mind and advice. He continued working for others till the ripe age of 84 till cancer took the better of him. He died a dignified death.

I drifted into life of my own after college. Joined the Army and enjoyed a well-accomplished career, raised a good family in an interactive environment and remained on fast track. My father continued in the same stride. Though aging, he displayed immense dynamism and was a powerhouse of energy, a source of inspiration for all. Though our parents could do with more comfort and care but he refused to shift to us due to his preoccupation with the adopted children. This set me thinking. I decided to spend time with him trying to understand him more.

Recollecting my school days, I realized how he had brought us up and at what to cost him—never passing on the financial or any other pressures down, creating an environment of growth with little interference, providing for all our necessities while denying quite some to himself. He did not acquire any property or transport, making it look easy for us. He got us into the front ranks of the system. His philanthropic work made him a person apart. He was a self-realized *karma yogi* in true sense. I felt all my achievements were but a humble patch on his selfless service to humanity. The values we adopted became synonymous with what we saw in him. All the efforts and principles of modern management we applied to bring up our children had been so easily accomplished by him with no formal knowledge. His model was perhaps warranted in that era. A revelation dawned on me when I realized that our offspring too had grown up on a similar path. The roots had firmed in, the growth was visible. I felt proud of him and relented for not understanding him earlier. How I wish I could communicate this to him now.

22

Growth of the Family Tree—An Experience

This material nature, which is one of my energies, is working under my direction; O son of Kunti, producing all moving and non-moving beings. Under its rule, this manifestation is created and annihilated again and again.
-Lord Krishana to Arjuna in the Bhagavad Gita [9.6]

It was already November. Remnants of summer were still holding out. Winter was waiting with its wings wide open, eager to take over. We had started on our trek rather early. The sun was yet to emerge from its night's slumber. The sky was clear. Mild breeze was flowing, making the pine trees whistle softly. There was chill in the air. The track was narrow and slippery due to the carpet of pine needles. The ambience was pure. We were heading for the ancient shrine of a local deity. The climb was steady, meandering through the dense forest, along the side of the hill, and finally emerging on the ridgeline. The shrine was now visible. It stood imposing, atop the hill in the distance. As we treaded forward, the skyline started changing its colour to crimson red, heralding the arrival of dawn. Soon the sun was out in its full glory; its rays dancing in the valley, splashing it with their golden hue at will. The view was breathtaking. We stood with our heads bowed in reverence to this manifestation of nature's splendour. Our mission was to pay obeisance and to seek blessings for our daughter who was due for a baby a few months hence. It was to be the first addition to our family from this generation. It was to be our baby's baby.

Growth is a sign of life. It is the movement forward, reflective of dynamic nature of the nature, be it intellectual, economic or even physical. All these are essential. Source of physical growth of a species is by procreation. It maintains genetic continuity. The process of procreation of infusing life in a cell fertilized by the sperm, growth of the cell into an embryo, its form and shape in the womb and its final delivery as a full-fledged replica of the parents is an awesome manifestation of the cosmic power. The chromosomes deciding the sex, the genes making each individual unique and traceable to its heritage, the process of growth progressing with precision in time and with pinpointed accuracy, and finally harmonious growth of all organs in keeping with overall growth is nothing but miraculous. It also confirms that there is a definite order and nature continues to exercise strict control all through. Viewed dispassionately, the process and the consequent result are too complicated to be fully explainable, yet too simple and universally common for all forms of life. It has been so from the very genesis of life. Applying all this to ourselves, we were enthralled by the immense power of the Creator. We anxiously waited for this miracle to happen to us also and smoothly.

It was a treat to watch the young mother to be, maturing gracefully, and going about scientifically and methodically in gathering all information about the much-needed requirements for her and the baby. The young father to be was also fully involved, enthusiastically understanding and learning his share of renewed responsibilities. Both of them had prepared the plan for acquisitions and actions for the event and executed it with finesse. For the expecting mother, prenatal checks, dietary precautions, physical exercises and the apparel to suit physical changes in the body had already been taken care of. For the baby, customized upper wear, lower wear, diapers, designer linen, toiletry requirements, transportation aids to carry the baby on person, for short distances, for longer ones and in a car, the dietary needs, the immunization schedule, and a variety of toys had been decided. It was a tedious experience for the mother, who had to exercise strict precautions in any intake including medicine. She had to be at peace and happy. All this would otherwise affect the baby in the womb. In spite of all this, her enthusiasm and excitement were reassuring. What pleasure and satisfaction a woman gets from her baby kicking from inside and how her protective instincts grow is indescribable. No wonder all women, even the most glamorous ones, knowing fully well about the harrowing time likely during this entire process want to experience motherhood. It is perhaps the greatest event in this universe. No one other than a mother can create life. She becomes the creator incarnate for her baby. Finally, our bundle of joy arrived.

It was a boy. So tiny and fragile that one could not be overcautious in handling it. He would change his resemblance every other day to his mother, father, and grand parents. It was perhaps the most photographed human being per capita hours of life. Even before he had tasted his first feed, his digital image had been flashed to friends and relations across the world. He appeared somewhat stunned by the sudden change of his environment from a cozy womb all to itself, to a huge room, with so many people vying for a look at him. But he learnt fast and got wise. He took complete charge of the environment. Entry in his room was regulated. The decibel level was strictly controlled. Sleep and wake up hours of the young mother went through a total shift. The baby settled for two to three hours cycles of feed and sleep. These cycles went on like a clock, only to be disturbed by occasional cries of the baby. The reasons for such outbursts were kept a close secret by the baby. Everyone was kept guessing. The mother had to find time in between all this for her own chores including rest and sleep. Notwithstanding this tight routine, the baby kept us all enthralled by its innocent looks, smiles and gestures. Its sensory and mental faculties were growing up well. This was reflected in its behaviour and responses. I heaved a sigh of relief and thanked the Creator for making all this happen.

As one observes more closely, total dependence of the human infant on its mother is conspicuous. Strangely, in spite of the fact that human life is considered to be the highest form of life, nature has chosen to make human infant the weakest and most vulnerable of nearly all living species. Even tiny birds, when hatched, start eating and digesting whatever their mother can find in her short outings. They learn to fly fast. Once they take their first flight, they learn to survive on their own. Offspring of marine life start swimming automatically. Offspring of wild life are protected, but only for short durations. One wonders as to what prompted God to make human child so dependent and for such a prolonged period, initially for physical care for mere survival and later for balanced and overall growth. In some cases, this period could extend well into adulthood. This is not easy for the parents. Demands of a modern child are extensive and specialized.

I was amazed to observe the transition of the young couple to parenthood. They adapted to this new role with ease and grace. Their life revolved around making the baby comfortable. It was a wonderful sight to see them taking turns to feed the baby, change his apparel, put him to sleep and even read him a story, irrespective of the fact that the child was only a few months old. Simultaneously, they commenced training of the baby, initially for focussing of the eyes and later for coordination of the limbs. The teaching aids then shifted to books with pictorial depictions and toys with visual and audio responses, and later to jigsaw puzzles to sharpen the mind. In short, there were a plethora of imaginative toys and games, and a library of books even before the child had entered the play way school. Once the baby started toddling, the aids changed. It was constantly outgrowing the aids. Musical rhymes and training videos were also cranked in to make all this interesting for the child. The effort of the parents was stupendous. Their sacrifice of personal comfort, their patience and perseverance was exemplary. Fortunately, the effect was encouraging. Positive results were already visible in the growth of the baby.

The child now goes to school. He is a sharp, playful child, who is fond of reading. He can be by himself for hours. Development of character values and fundamental traits is visible. He needs rationale for what is expected of him. Hence, it is a two-way traffic with him. I feel he is on the right track to grow up to be a good human being.

Once the dust settled down, one could sit back and reflect on the impact of this phenomenal event on our lives. It was a revelation that our daughter had grown up so much to become a mother, that too an efficient one. We still considered her to be a baby of the family. This addition to our family had changed the entire equation of relationships. Overnight every one was one generation older. Grandfather! Though majestic in status, it sounded as if one needed a stick for support. The new born cemented the bond within the families. Everyone rallied to share and participate in the events. The child became a replay of our own lives as young parents. I wanted to pamper the child and do all that I missed doing for my own children. In fact, at times I felt guilty. I, for certain, had not shared even a fraction of the load in my turn. I am also certain that we had not been so elaborate in bringing up the children. While we insisted on character values and basic tenets of life, but we were far from paying so much attention and in such great detail as this generation had done. But our model also was successful under the given circumstances and the means available at that time. Maybe current pressures demand one to be so meticulous. I may add, effort of this young couple is not unique, entire current generation is seized with this requirement and is coping with it in a similar manner.

Looking at our grandson, a strange thought crossed my mind. It was to predict about his future. Not as in a horoscope, but to visualize what could be in store for him. Before I could do so, instinctively my own life started flashing in front of me as if on fast forward starting from the earliest that I could remember. I recalled the toil and effort as a student; the pressure of examinations; palpitation at the time of results; my joining the profession; the challenges that I had to face at each step; my urge to excel and therefore the pressure to work hard; my strengths and weaknesses; my successes and failures; all the happiness and pain; my retirement and life thereafter. This entire replay was staring at my face. Although my life, relatively a successful model, but all this for what? Eventually to shed apparel of this withering body and pick up a new one. I don't really know of which species. All about futility of human life. And about the sages who undertook lifelong penance to get out of this cycle of life and after life. But how can I share all this with my grandson, who is on the threshold of life, bubbling with energy to learn, work hard and do well. How can I even discourage him with these thoughts? Won't I sound selfish? It might make him feel that having lived and enjoyed my own life, I am being pessimistic for him. So I decided to keep these strange thoughts to myself and allow him to grow and learn for himself. In any case, having been born, what can one really do but live. So why not live positively? I have no answer for this. I can only wish him the best and pray for His blessings for him.

23

Whither God

I am the creator. I am the past, the present and the future.
-Lord Krishna in the Bhagavad Gita

Existence of God was often the subject of discussion with my grandfather in my formative years. My grandfather would offer intriguing arguments not only explaining His existence but His all-pervading presence. As he explained, we are all actors on the stage of life and the show goes on. But no show can go on without the director. It is His cosmic presence that dictates all actions or inactions. I often retorted, seeking scientific justification for the existence of this director and the rationale for existence of the evil mind in spite of God being in complete control of the universe. To this, the patriarch would at times go on the defensive and seek a counterargument from me, asking if He did not exist, how did the nature manifest its powers; how did the sun exist and radiate its energy; what makes the earth rotate; how does human and animal life exist; how do seeds sprout to a sapling, flowers bloom, etc. While my grandfather would quote from religious scriptures and mythology, I would back my arguments with scientific inventions and laws of physics and chemistry that claimed to solve some of the riddles of life. I must state here that I was neither an atheist nor a blind believer. I respected the basic values for being a good human being, but my curiosity to learn about the real God goaded me to plunge deeper into this thought and seek the answers. Since there was no pre-determined solution and solid evidence available for the existence of God, my grandfather smiled patiently and offered to adjourn the issue till I grew up and gained more experience of life.

Unfortunately, the second innings of the scheduled discussion, with me fortified with wisdom and experience of life, never took place. I drifted into life of my own, joined the Army, and became a professional soldier, committed and busy. I rose up to a good rank, and raised a good family. But my grandfather did not wait. He left for his heavenly abode. Somewhere in the din of life, I even lost track of my side of the argument. An imperceptible change had taken place in me. Having experienced many a facet of life, I had become a firm believer. The subject itself remained buried under my subconscious mind.

Recently, I read the famous work, *Autobiography* of a *Yogi* by Swami Paramhansa Yoganand. Having spent a long time practising yogic life and experiencing spiritual bliss in meditation, the yogi asked his guru, Swami Yukteswar, "Sir, I want to know when I shall find God?" To this, the guru replied, "You have found him." But the yogi was not convinced. The guru, who was known to have spiritual powers, smiled and said, "I am not sure if you are expecting a venerable personage adorning a throne in some antiseptic corner of the cosmos. I see, however, that you are imagining that the possession of miraculous powers is knowledge of God. One might have the whole universe and find the Lord elusive still. Spiritual advancement is not measured by one's outward powers, but only by the depth of His bliss in meditation. Ever new joy is God. He is inexhaustible; as you continue meditation during the years, He will beguile you with an infinite ingenuity..."[1]

My earlier years and the sittings with my grandfather flashed back vividly across my mind. I found some more answers to the long-pending issue, the proof of God's existence. It is evident that there can be no better proof than to experience God personally. However, this does not come easy. It requires lifelong dedication and devotion to the Lord, and still one may not be found worthy of His revelations. Till then, one may continue to be a good human being. Lesser mortals like me may remain satisfied with the proof of God's existence by default, in witnessing the marvel of His creation. Equipped with this logic, I am now ready to continue the discussions on the subject with my grandson. Unfortunately, I have to wait for a while, as he has just started going to school.

---

1. *Autobiography of a Yogi*, Paramhansa Yogananda, Facsimile Edition, 1997, pp 154, 155.

24

Once upon a Time

It is easy to quit smoking.
I have done it a hundred times.
- Mark Twain

Once upon a time, I was extremely popular. I was considered to be contemporary; a style, a fashion. I was the darling of professionals and amateurs alike—for professionals, to augment their veracity and promote their image, and for amateurs, to boost their confidence and enhance their personality. I would equally befit a dashing hero rescuing a pretty maiden, a matinee idol, a detective to lend credence to his poise and mystique, a philosopher to unleash his mind to soar to lofty heights, a tragic hero to brood on his lovelorn heart, and even a villain to make him look more villainous. It was not uncommon to see many celebrities as my close associates, ever identifying with me as an inseparable companion. Many impressionable minds would fondly cherish the indelible imprints that I would leave upon them through these celebrities. I was often associated with a macho image, bravado, art, a creative mind, celebrations, romanticism, tragedy, depression, and with affairs of the heart. People would seek my indulgence to relax, de-stress, or even to fill their time. No specific time or occasion was required; they just needed an excuse to be with me. I had become the second nature, a habit to many. That was my golden era. No wonder, I was the heartthrob of the advertisers. I was not only lapped up for advertisements but had also acquired some hypnotic power to influence minds of the masses. I became the preferred platform for launch of many mega events. I had social acceptability and was flashed all over with pride. People from all walks of life would indulge in me innovatively; be it through the media of a cigarette, cigar, or a pipe, or even through some of the oriental-adapted versions of the ancient art of smoking like beedi, hookah and the like. Yes, that's what they called me, 'smoking', or 'smoking a cigarette', in the generic sense. Little did I know that the very wave of popularity that I was riding and the iconic cult that I had created were to become my bête noir and the cause of my downfall. All this gives rise to some issues. What exactly is smoking? How did it become so popular? What caused the paradigm shift in the thinking mind to suddenly drop it like a hot brick? And finally, what impact does it leave on those who patronize it?

Smoking is a simple act of inhaling and exhaling of fumes of burning tobacco in a cigarette, pipe, or cigar. A cigarette looks deceptively simple. Just a blend of tobacco leaves, shredded and loosely wrapped in a paper tube. The stem, stalk and remaining bits of tobacco leaf are also shredded and mixed with tobacco as fillers. And finally, a filter at the mouth end. All these are highly engineered products designed for sustained and consistent delivery of nicotine.[1] The tobacco mix comprises of two types of tobacco leaves blended in specified proportion for the desired taste and effect. The fillers are added to save on the wastage. Flavours are added to counter the foul taste caused by the fillers. The filter is made of cellulose acetate. It is densely packed and cools the gases thus facilitating inhaling. It also arrests a portion of 'tar', a toxic chemical component of the fumes. Finally, there are a variety of additives designed for specified effects. Moisturizers are used to enhance the shelf life, sugar to make the fumes appear milder, and vanilla, chocolate and some juices for aroma and taste. Nicotine, tar and carbon monoxide are the key chemicals released by a cigarette.

Nicotine is present in liquid form in tobacco. On combustion, it evaporates and is inhaled along with the smoke. Within a few seconds, it reaches the brain and stimulates the nervous system, thereby increasing the heartbeat and blood pressure. Once smoking is over, the nicotine content in the blood falls, causing an addictive craving for a refill as in the case of drugs.[2] Tar is the particle matter of the tobacco. In its condensate form, tar is a sticky brown substance (filled with chemicals), which can stain smoker's fingers and teeth. Tar attacks the DNA and is the key cause of lung cancer. Carbon monoxide is the gaseous by-product of incomplete combustion. It absorbs oxygen from the smoker's respiratory system, thereby reducing the supply of oxygen to the blood. This gives rise to a variety of cardiovascular disorders. Besides these chemicals, there are a large

---

1. :www.ciggyfree.com
2. http://www.pauldouglass.co.uk

number of other toxic by-products like aldehydes, ammonia, prussic acid, etc., which affect the nervous system.

The fashion, style, and aura of movie stars influence the naïve to take up smoking. Many famous celebrities of the past too used cigars, cigarettes, or pipes as a part of their image, eg., Winston Churchill. Movie stars strongly influence impressionable teenagers, who are the most vulnerable as they take up smoking either to emulate their parents, movie stars, for a macho image, as a reflection of their rebellious mind, or merely for imaginary thrill of entering adulthood. As a result, smoking grew unchallenged.

Romanticism of the puff lasted as long as ignorance persisted. Popularity of smoking resulted in increase in diseases and health disorders. This realization made the societies to react sharply. Massive awareness campaigns were launched across the globe by various organizations and governments. They came down heavily to enforce curbs on smoking advertisements, creating awareness of the grievous harm caused by the chemicals being inhaled, and enforced regulations to display cautions, warnings and even the content of nicotine and tar on the packaging. Even higher taxes have been imposed as deterrence. To safeguard against passive smoking, smoking areas have been segregated. In many cases, bans have been imposed on smoking in public places. All this has had a salutary effect. The number of casual smokers has gone down drastically. Whatever cases remain are the deliberate ones, those who take a calculated risk and possibly want to quit but are unable to do so due to addiction. Fresh cases, mostly teenagers, continue to add up but their numbers have dwindled. To help the willing, many help lines have mushroomed to offer counselling and psychological help. Now smoking is a rare sight in public; it possibly carries a social stigma. Awareness about passive smoking has added a new dimension to shun a smoking joint.

In spite of massive reduction in the number of smokers, the number of patients reeling under the lasting impact is still large. Cancer institutes are full, thanks to the miniscule presence of even less than 10 mg of tar in a cigarette, which is sufficient to initiate this wretched disease in smokers and even in passive smokers. Cases of high cholesterol, blood pressure and cardiovascular diseases are on the increase, courtesy presence of less than one mg per cigarette of nicotine. Carbon monoxide, one of the most poisonous gases, is inhaled as a complimentary by-product due to partial combustion of tobacco. As if this was not enough, persistent smoking has adverse effects on the eyes, respiratory system, neurological system, and normal growth of the human body. The worst effect is that a smoker is in a constant state of stupor. But in spite of all the awareness campaigns and regulations, smoking continues to exist, and even grow as an escapade, or challenge, or an imaginary aid. I recall that I too have had a fling with smoking long way back.

My first puff was incidental when I was 11. My father, then a chain smoker, asked me to dispose of the butt. I chose to try out a puff. I choked and suddenly felt guilty. I hid in a dark corner and had to be retrieved by my sister. My fling with smoking started when I was a young officer, a fitness buff and a teetotaler. In a party, I overheard a passing conversation between some pretty ladies that a cigarette held in style added to one's personality. I was not even certain of the context. Nonetheless, the observation remained stuck with me till I decided to give it a try. Smoking would leave a foul taste, so I would brush my teeth many times. Light brown stains appeared on the insides of my teeth. Keen to retain my looks, I would scratch these off with a blade. But gradually, similar stains appeared on my fingertips. I would scrub my fingers hard. I continued with the experiment, torn between the dilemma to undo any adverse effect. With time, this activity, which I had undertaken only on a trial basis, had started growing on me. I soon graduated from a few cigarettes in a day to rolling my own cigarettes. This was much harder a tobacco. I would finish a pouch of tobacco in a few days. By now, its impact on my stamina had also started showing. I received the first jolt when I came a poor sixth in a 400-metre event in formation. I was the runner-up the previous year. I had to struggle to maintain my fitness level. The final push came when I lost in a preliminary round to a far inferior player in the formation squash tournament. I was huffing and puffing half way through the game. That was it, I decided. I quit that day.

With that, my fledgling career of smoking came to an end in less than four years. Maybe I had waited too long to decide. Maybe I needed those jolts to make me quit. But finally, better sense prevailed. Possibly, the motivation to excel in sports and my urge for physical fitness had come to my rescue. I did lose some precious years, where instead of moving forward, I had to struggle to stay afloat. In hindsight, I feel it was still not so heavy a price to pay. I got away with it lightly in spite of all this happening during the so-called golden era of smoking. I have been off it for four decades and fortunately have never had the urge to try it again.

25

The Battle Which I Nearly Lost

Nothing is impossible. You have to have the will to do it.

The year was 1971. I was posted as an instructor in the prestigious National Defence Academy (NDA). Besides furtherance in profession, NDA offered ample facilities for adventure and sports. I was an ardent sportsman, so I pursued my favourite sports with vigour. Although I had the privilege to represent India in an international yachting regatta, my first love continued to be squash. I enjoyed the sport thoroughly. It was a treat to compete with the cadets; some of them had already excelled at the junior nationals. Incidentally, I had yet another feather in my cap. In the current ranking, I was number one in the squash ladder in the academy. As a follow-up, I was called for trials leading to selection for the services squash team. The tournament was being held at the School of Artillery, Deolali. It was an opportunity which I was eagerly looking forward to.

Keeping my form and fitness in view, I was quite confident of doing well. So I packed my bags and departed for Deolali. Little did I know that my life would take an unexpected turn there.

Instead of a smooth sailing, which should have been in the normal course, things started going awry right from the very beginning. The train journey was not comfortable at all. I did not have a proper berth, and there was too much smoke in the compartment, thanks to the steam engines which were still in service on some sections. To make the matters worse, it started raining and became unusually cold. I was not geared for all this. I had involuntarily inhaled several lungful of coal dust and was shivering involuntarily. As a cumulative result, I felt feverish and caught bad cold. Some funny wheezing sounds also started emanating from my chest. My breathing became heavy. All this on the eve of the strenuous tournament ahead! It was not an ominous sign. Though it was not the case of life and death, but I did have my image at stake. I wanted to put up my best in the tournament. It was all very unnerving. I felt I was being given a raw deal by nature. A serious handicap was being thrust upon me. I hoped all this would disappear after some rest.

Unfortunately, arrangements at the other end were also not too comfortable. It was quite some time before I could find a room and settle down. Feeling of well-being had disappeared. Wheezing continued unabated. But my willpower still had the better of me. I brushed aside these symptoms and adopted my earlier tried out approach. When not feeling well, sweat out. My treatment kit, the skipping rope, was right with me. Unfortunately, this formula did not succeed this time. In fact, the matters took a turn for the worse. My breath was choking. I was coughing incessantly. I had to do something about it; I had to fill my lungs with sufficient oxygen. I discovered a suitable posture. It was the crouching position, sitting on the edge of the bed, bent forward. I remained in that posture almost throughout the night. Finally, there was some respite and I could manage to catch sleep in the early hours. I did not really know what exactly was happening. Was it something serious or was it a temporary phenomenon? After having rested for a few hours, I put all these questions away and thought of the round-robin matches in the evening. I was still confident that once I entered the court, I would be fine. The idea of pulling out did not even cross my mind. I decided to rest and take my chances. I did get some medicines, but these did not help much. On the contrary, my heartbeat increased phenomenally. I could hear loud thudding sound inside. It was palpitation. I did not really understand the gravity of what all I was undergoing. All this I was to learn and in good detail later to my utter dismay.

In the evening, I played my match. Fortunately, it was relatively easy. Drawing upon my reserve of energy and with shear willpower, I won, though panting and coughing throughout. All this was happening to a person who was known for his stamina. Anyway, I hung on for two more days and played some tougher matches, won some and lost some. The performance was acceptable but nowhere near my actual potential. My condition continued to deteriorate. The nights were still sleepless, and mostly spent in the famous crouching posture. I think I had stretched my willpower and mental courage to the edge. This bravado was bordering on foolhardiness. In fact, it was so from day one. I wonder how I drew the courage and strength to last three tough days. My ego notwithstanding, I felt it was time to see the doctor. He declared that I was undergoing a fully blown attack of asthma. I was required to be hospitalized. On my request and risk, he allowed me to go back to NDA and get admitted there. To everyone's surprise, the subdued hero returned breathless, chastised and humbled by nature.

I was hospitalized in the military hospital the next morning. After some tests and medication, my chest started clearing. Finally, the congestion disappeared. My breathing became normal and the wheezing sound too disappeared What a relief it was for me! As if some burden had been taken off my chest. Although this trauma had lasted for a few days only but appeared to be a lifetime. The breathing system, though innocuous, is the lifeline of a human being. It continues to function all the time, unobtrusively and reflexively. As long it remains so, it is good. Come slightest hindrance in this passage, the reflexive part disappears. Now deliberate effort is required to breathe. Imagine all this for every breath and throughout. I shivered at the very thought of my bitter experience. Was it over, or was it only the beginning? Only time would tell. I was soon discharged from the hospital but not before being placed in a low medical category. I was given an advisory to avoid excessive physical stress, high altitude, dust, pollens, etc. I was given medicines which would take care of the problem on recurrence. It was not curative. I was to be reviewed regularly, and could be declared fit, if at all, only in steps, provided my medical parameters like isnophilia count, vital capacity of the lungs, wheezing sound, etc., became normal. It appeared to be a long drawn affair. How all this was going to happen was not known. Ironically, the onus to become fit seemed to have fallen squarely in my lap but with no means and wherewithal to solve the riddle. I was groping for answers knowing fully well the implications of all this on my career and lifestyle.

It was time to introspect. I learnt that asthma is a chronic disease caused by inflammation of the breathing passages or airways of the lungs. In case of asthma, these airways become highly sensitive to environmental triggers like smoke, dust, pollens, etc. The airways become narrow and produce mucus, which constricts the passage further. This leads to wheezing, coughing and choking, and finally to laboured breathing. I learnt that there are as many as 200 allergen that can trigger asthma. The sensitivity of an individual to a particular allergy could be isolated, though by an elaborate process. This involved injecting each type of allergy and then observing the reactions. Obviously, it was not only long drawn but a dangerous process, as it could make one vulnerable to a new allergy. It was unbelievable that in allopathic science, asthma cannot be cured completely; though it can be managed to enable one to lead an active life. The common treatment was to administer steroids in various forms, viz., oral, inhalers or by intravenous injections depending upon the intensity of the attack. These act as bronchi dilators. The relief would last for a while. Pity is that if taken regularly, one develops immunity, leading to consumption of higher doses of medicine. Most patients end up with inhalers. These invariably caused palpitation of the heart. In case the attack was not stemmed in the early stage, one might have to be put on oxygen. Chronic patients normally keep oxygen cylinders handy. Even learning about all this was giving me goose pimples. In short, one was at the mercy of the allergen, which could erupt at will and cause the trigger. I was totally disillusioned. What was to happen to my sports, my career? Was I to change my total lifestyle because of some stupid allergen? My gut reaction was a big no. Though I was not armed with detailed answers, I resolved to find some solutions, which obviously lay outside the allopathic domain. These could be in ayurvedic, homeopathic, nature therapy, or even unorthodox treatments. Formal medical channel considered all these alternates as quackery and therefore would not endorse. It was a catch 22 situation. I took my decision. This was to be my battle; my personal and psychological battle. The battle against a very slimy enemy; the battle which I could not afford to lose.

Discussions with the locals revealed that the climate prevailing in that area was conducive to asthmatic attacks. Anyone susceptible to this problem was bound to have an aggravated situation. This must have been so in my case as well. I was to recall this later. Unfortunately, after my initial recovery, the problem still continued. I would often have wheezing and feel breathless. I had to spend many a sleepless night in that wretched crouching posture. Psychologically, I would not like to be seen by anyone in that position. It hurt my dignity. My wife was a great support, helpful and reassuring, yet unobtrusive. After due deliberations, the problem had to be kept in check and not allowed to go out of control. For this, allopathy was the only answer. Accordingly, an appropriate steroid formed part of my first-aid kit. I would swallow the medicine on the first indication, and taper it off at the first opportunity. This became a way of my life. Next, we addressed the dietary controls. After many a hit and trials, it revealed that stomach held the key to any solution if at all. I resorted to simple and light food, early dinner, no fries, no afternoon nap, removed some of my favourite dishes from my menu, kept the stomach light to ensure that my digestive system functioned well. Some alcohol, yes. It helped dilation of airways. All this had a salutatory effect. It was time to restart my exercises and sports.

We were now scouting for the alternate therapy to eradicate the problem. We chose the multiple paths of homeopathy and ayurvedic concoctions. Although these did help, some wheezing continued, particularly at higher stress levels. It was time to turn to basics and seek answers in the nature's cure. First step was to learn yoga. Hunt for a good yoga teacher culminated finally in Pune. This added to my travails as I had to commute for nearly an hour either way for a 45-minute session. I learnt basic yoga poses and asnas, and the fundamentals of *pranayam*. Having achieved reasonable proficiency in three weeks or so, I was to continue on my own. For my specific problem of asthma, the teacher guided me to a yoga specialist centre in Lonavala, an hour away by train from Pune. The effort was getting colossal, I was getting frustrated, but my father inspired me to take this plunge. He even offered to accompany me. We commuted to Lonavala every morning using multiple transports.

In the yogic ashram at Lonavala, I was taught *pranayam* and the *kriyas* for cleansing the breathing passages. With *pranayam*, my lung capacity increased phenomenally. My normal pulse rate and breathing rate dropped. The *kriyas* were tough to learn. These were *vaman dhoti, vastra dhoti* and *neti dhoti. Vaman dhoti* was the easiest as it involved drinking jugs full of saline water and gradually throwing it out by sticking a finger in the throat.

Besides physically flushing the inners, force of the exercise made blood rush to the extremities of the body, which normally does not happen. *Vastra dhoti* involved swallowing a sterilized piece of muslin cloth approximately five inches in width and six yards in length and then pulling it out. This cleaned the entire passage to the stomach like the barrel of a gun. This was the toughest to learn. Finally, *neti dhoti* involved pouring water in one nostril and taking out from the other, and also passing a rubber pipe from one and taking out from the other. Having achieved basic proficiency in the *kriyas* in one week's time, I was to continue on my own.

Fortunately for me, the academy was closed on account of term break. So I could spare time for my above ventures. All these activities not only restored my vitality but made me more athletic. A fresh glow appeared on my face. I owed it to yoga and *pranayam*. Yoga is not merely a set of exercises; it is a combination of prayers and physical activity. It gives inner happiness, a feeling of contentment. *Pranayam* helps one to regulate breathing. It vitalizes the lungs and breathing passages. I don't know whether all my medical parameters were meeting the standards of the allopathic science or not, but I was feeling healthy and had become more athletic and energetic. I was participating in sports with renewed vigour. But I never left my guard and continued to take the precautions against this slimy enemy. It was now time for my first medical review.

The medical specialist looked at my blood test reports. It seemed to be within limits. Then he checked my chest for any congestion, he did not find any. He seemed to be more tense than me. He looked for wheezing sounds in the bronchi tubes at the extremities of the chest and at the back. Finally, he smiled. I thought he was going to clear me. On the contrary, the triumphant smile was for having heard an occasional gurgle in the small bronchi tubes at the back. Maybe the *vamna dhoti* and *vastra dhoti kriyas* could not reach the small tubes. He declared that I had shown phenomenal improvement, but status quo was to be maintained. I was disappointed, as I was feeling fitter than earlier. Maybe this gurgle existed in even those who were not a victim of this disease. Maybe I had this all along, as I recall a bronchitis situation when I was 14. I wondered why the specialist was now seeing all this with a magnifying glass. Did he expect a patient to bounce back as a superman, or was he deliberately doing me down? Later, I was to learn that the specialist was aware of my recovery and return to yet a higher level of fitness and without much help from them. This was news to them as other cases were not responding like this. He wanted to make it a watertight case, lest he be questioned. Hence, this blatant display of meticulous professionalism.

Come next review, I was wiser. Thanks to *pranayam*, I could hold my breath for nearly two minutes. Rest everything being normal, when I found the specialist fishing for clues in the extreme tubes which were perhaps absent this time, I would hold my breath and only heave using my diaphragm. This would primarily be from the main tubes. There was no sound. The physician was rattled and fired the last salvo. I was put through yet another test, test of vital capacity of the lungs. The report was very good. This time he genuinely smiled. My lung capacity was nearly 50 per cent higher than normal level. He finally relented and upgraded me by one step. Rest is history.

I was fully upgraded faster than scheduled in the next station, and continued to be so for the rest of my service of more than three decades and till now. I braved hazardous weather, extreme climates and super-high altitudes even without acclimatization with confidence and comfort. It was talk of the town. I had learnt my lesson; never take your foe lightly, particularly, when he is invisible and unpredictable. The essence has been to continue with yoga, *pranayam*, hard exercise and sweat, be it by squash or gym. I continued with the *kriyas*, but only for a few years, thereafter only *vaman dhoti*. In fact, my entire family learnt and still practices *vaman dhoti* as the first line of defense when bad cold is even imminent. Notwithstanding all this, my emergency kit has always remained intact and with me with one theme: should this enemy show even the slightest sign, strike hard. Nip the evil in the bud. And this is true for all enemies.

26

On Squash

Squash is like boxing with racquets...
- Jonah Barrington

The setting was perfect. Imposing buildings and sprawling lawns of the university campus offered a rare blend of architectural grandeur and matching verdancy. Central roads were majestically lined by shady and flowering trees like mango, banyan, peepul, gulmohar, Indian laburnum a la amaltas, mahogany, etc., while link roads were besotted by medium-sized trees and bushes including golden dewdrops, Indian ginseng or ashwagandha, champa, mahua, and oleander. The lawns boasted of a rare variety of flowering plants and bushes. In this exotic specter, young scholars were strolling at leisure, some were moving on bikes, appearing casual but focussed, relaxed but purposeful; lending an air of dignity and hope. Hope for the future; hope resting on their relentless pursuit of knowledge, on their energy and on their power of youth. The ambience was reassuring and the atmosphere serene and literary.

We had come to the campus of Banaras Hindu University, bubbling with enthusiasm and expectations. It was for the future of our son who had been selected through a tough competition to pursue engineering studies. But my enthusiasm was soon ebbing. I became skeptic, subdued and somewhat unsure. I was thinking about the hostel facilities, which I felt, left much to be desired. These were not measuring to the literary standards of the institution. I felt apprehensive as my son was to live in these environs for four years. Subconsciously, I also felt guilty for what all I had access to in my own turn, when I had joined the National Defence Academy as an officer cadet. I was shaken out of my reverie by familiar echoes emanating from the squash courts nearby. Stupefied by this surprise bonanza, we drifted towards these like robots. We found some university level players playing. Soon I was in the court making an impression. Later my son also proved his mettle in court. He was promptly lapped up as a potential member of the university team. This transformed our perceptions. Our son, who too had been quiet, holding back his emotions, instantaneously fell in love with that place. Nothing else mattered thereafter. Squash had changed it all. So what exactly is squash? And what did it mean to me?

Squash is perhaps the most absorbing and challenging racquet sport. It has derived its name from 'squashability' of the hollow spherical rubber ball used in this sport. Though the origin of the sport dates back to the 19th Century in the United Kingdom, it remained the preserve of select group of upper middle class and Army officers. With the opening of public courts, it acquired wider access and became immensely popular around the 1970s. Today, it is considered fashionable for the corporate world executive to be a squash player. In India, squash is still not widely accessible, except to an extent in the metros, but is vibrant in nearly all the military stations.

Squash requires a well-lit indoor court approximately 32 feet by 21 feet in size with a high roof and wooden flooring. It is normally played between two players who are positioned on the same side of the court taking the strike alternatively with squash racquets. The aim is to 'kill' the ball after hitting on the front wall or to force the opponent to default. The ball can be struck directly or off the side within the defined boundaries. The sports gear, particularly the racquet, has undergone a revolutionary change. Innovations in the design and material of the racquet have resulted in introduction of metallic and graphite racquets. It has led to increase of the surface area. The weight has come down from 250 gms of the erstwhile laminated wood material to 110 gms. This has impacted on the speed and character of the game. Another revolutionary change has been ushered in by the introduction of glass courts, facilitating mass viewing and wider media coverage.

My first exposure to squash was more than four and half decades back. I was in the final term in the National Defence Academy when I chanced upon this sport by a mere coincidence. I stood mesmerized watching a game in progress. Once inside the court, I felt as if I belonged there. I developed an instant liking for it. It was like love at first sight. This response, though instinctive, was not totally without a rationale. There were many reasons for it which I analysed later. I felt induction into squash could be relatively easy. Unlike other individual sports, it did not require great skills to begin with. Given a reasonable aptitude, initial phase of the learning curve could be fairly steep and encouraging. The court size is small and the ball bouncing back keeps the pace fast and makes the game interesting. For me, this phase was a real confidence builder. I relished hitting the ball hard. The noise of the impact resounding in the enclosure gave a feeling of power. Thrilled by initial success, I decided to pursue this as my main sport. Little did I realize that the plateau of the learning curve was to set in rather soon, as if waiting around the corner. Apparently, simplicity of the game had ended there. Much more was required to improve further.

Further improvement demanded high level of concentration, sharp reflexes, strong forearm and wrist action, tremendous agility and loads of stamina. I devised my own techniques to build up on my attributes. These attributes are vital prerequisites for a decent level of proficiency. I observed that squash is akin to boxing. Fireworks start from the word 'go'. One cannot take his eyes off the ball even for a second. There is no time to think. One has to act, and act fast as the ball comes back at a much faster pace. Total reflexive time, that is, the time elapsed between sensory to motor nerves to action, drops sharply. One has to develop auto reflexes. Simply put, squash demands a player to have the stamina of a horse and the agility of a tiger with innate patience to create an opportunity and pounce for a 'kill'. I tried to master the basic shots, which actually are very few; parallels, cross, lobs and drops; played both off-fore and back hands, directly or off the walls. Of these, I found forehand to be my strong point, as I was not so confident of the drop shots.

I learnt that it is the court craft in application of these shots in various combinations which stretched the level to a scorching pace and accuracy. The same court now starts appearing much larger in size.

With time and experience, my game improved. The passion too continued unabated. Now was the time to focus on the most vital factor of the game, the opponent. First, I felt one had to be constantly vigilant about the position and direction of movement of the opponent. For this, it was essential to enhance one's own vision by creating the ability to watch or sense from the corner of the eyes, without taking eyes off the front wall. This facilitates surprising the opponent and keeps one from being surprised.

Next, one had to innovate shots to outwit the opponent and create openings while rallying to keep the ball in play. Every player builds up on his attributes and develops his own style. Some are predominantly strong in touch game, while most modern players thrive on power and stamina. I realized that it was vital to control the centre of the court and the pace of the game. Deception in execution of a shot was yet another factor which could unnerve the opponent. For this, one has to reduce the swing, and delay the shot till as late as possible, thereby reducing the response time for the opponent. A strong wrist action had to be developed for this. Other shots which I developed were killing on full volleys, acute angled off wall kills and an occasional mix of even half volleys. Application of these has to be planned to counter each opponent case by case. There is no universal formula common to all. Only if one could read the mind of the opponent and modify one's game plan to play on his psyche, half the battle would be won. A tall order, but it is possible with practice and with the help of a good coach. Fortified with all these analyses, I was ready to reflect on what did squash mean to me.

Initially, I came to like squash perhaps thinking that it was an easy sport to pick up. This liking graduated to become a second nature, rather a way of life for me. There were many reasons for this. My stamina, agility and good wrist action gave me an instant edge. I could pack plenty of exercise in a very short time. A good match of squash hardly lasts more than an hour. Being an indoor sport, it is independent of time and vagaries of weather. Psychologically, I liked it more as this was the first sport I could excel in, and pursue in my own time and pace. All this suited me ideally as I could interweave my workout with an interesting game in minimal time with no elaborate arrangements and with no interference in my profession.

I was fortunate to continue to play unhindered all along, except when deployed in field areas. And I am continuing to do so even in my retirement. This long journey of over four and a half decades of squash has not been totally free from any ripples. More often than not, I was advised to respect my age and hang the racquet, when I was just 40 and looked all set to rise in the Army. For that one also had to remain medically fit. This was bolstered by an oft-quoted example of a particular officer who died while playing squash. I deliberated and chose to continue. My logic was and still is that one is the best judge of his own level of fitness and has to be wise enough to control his pace. I also believe that there would always be some indicator which must be promptly attended to. I did get some reverse Ts in my ECG, but these straightened on the tread mill during the test. Even the echocardiogram test result was very good. That gave me a carte blanche to continue undeterred. Later, an arthritic problem in my left knee erupted unexpectedly. This was overcome with innovative efforts, much to the surprise of the orthopaedics. Was this due to squash or for squash? I don't know for sure, but squash did influence my thoughts and actions.

Squash has given me much more than I could have asked for. I have continued to be physically fit and youthful. But I seek no guarantees for the future. As regards my level of proficiency, I did not reach any dizzy heights, but I did excel at club and the armed forces level. In my squash memory, I recall with nostalgia, when in a military station open, I lost in the finals in a five setter to none other than my son. It was also a moment of pride. The baton was passing and a legacy setting in. I was a brigadier then. I continued with the same gusto and later won both the open and veteran's squash in another station. I was a two star general then. I am fortunate to be playing fairly well even now as I write this. I continue to have some innovative shots in my armory and am still a threat to young players. Playing with the young keeps me youthful. Squash has also been the panacea for my ailments. The moment I am in the court, I become totally fit, and the ailment starts to disappear reflexively. Squash is no longer a mere sport; it continues to be a way of life for me, if not an obsession.

27

Walkie-Talkie of Gold Mohar

You love God's creations, you love God
-Anon

Walkie-talkie of Gold Mohar. Yes, that's what her official name was when she emerged majestically from the leather jacket of the courier. She swept past us on all fours, made a few laps of the lawn and sauntered into the house confidently, gracing each and every corner, familiarizing with the new environs. Her pure golden colour, perfect build and graceful movements held us spellbound. Finally, she condescended to look at us and meet each one of us, wagging her tail, making a variety of quizzical noises and licking whatever and whoever came her way. She was to be the new member of our family, a two-month old Labrador, procured after some discussions and research. She brought in an aura of warmth and affection. Our daughter spontaneously christened her 'Summer'. The name just suited her personality.

She was dynamic and compulsively warm and affectionate. She too liked the new name as she started responding to the same without inhibition.

Although we had pets all along, it was our first experience with a Labrador. Summer grew up with a difference. In spite of formal obedience and specialized training, schedules for walks and reluctant runs, exercises and prescribed diet, she didn't lose her originality and natural naughtiness. Playful as she was, she would keep us occupied by her intelligent responses and mischievous tricks of trying to catch the running water from the pipe, running after butterflies, picking low-hanging mangoes and oranges from the trees, looking at the revolving fan with surprise and so on. She developed a penchant for toys. Both our children would invariably shower her with an enviable variety of toys mostly purchased from abroad. Summer figured on top for the shopping list of our son and his family during their trips back home from New York and our daughter from her sojourns the world over along with her husband on board his merchant navy ships.

Summer had been acquired with an understanding to be brought up under the control of my wife with oblique warnings to me not to pamper and spoil her. She grew up well, taking to the training as second nature. She could search and retrieve things with an uncanny intelligence. Though she acquired her full size in less than a year, but at heart, she remained an affectionate child. It was at this stage that we observed distinct change in her. She became not only attached but very possessive of me. It would be a problem for anyone else to take her leash if I was around. Being in the Army, I had to be away for long times. However, she perhaps had some sixth sense and would be at the gate even when my staff car was miles away. She would insist on sitting close to my feet and tag along from room to room after me. She could sense any signs of stress or tension, and after staring for sometime, she would quietly move, try to reach up with her front paws and lick my face. It was her way of conveying that all would be well. If I ever raised my voice, beyond the decibel level set by her arbitrarily, she would repeat the same procedure, as if appeasing not to have been the cause of the perceived anger. She took the place as the third child in our family. Natural offspring being away from the nest and on their own, she became our focus.

In due course of time, I retired and we moved to a flat in another station. Summer found it very unusual for me to be at home and available to her much longer than usual. She has got used to the new environs. We find her least demanding. She has become the darling of the neighbours and the children dote on her. She is the 12th fielder in the local cricket team, and relishes drives in our new car, enjoying the comfort of the rear seat, moving from window to window at will. We are obliged with occasional invitations from our friends, courtesy Summer, as their children too have fallen for her.

At times, I sit back and observe the enigma called Summer. She has given us so much, seeking and expecting nothing in return. She continues to be dynamic, keeps our spirits up, has affectionate and innocent looks to offer, and sees you straight in the eyes. It will be extremely difficult to falter from the values that we have and practice, lest one is not able to look in her eyes. She has helped us to remain on course. Her selflessness is a true reflection of a *karma yogi.* She is more human than human beings. We are overwhelmed with her presence. I am sure she understands our feelings. Knowing well about the short canine lifespan, we would be naïve to seek her longevity beyond the natural. However, we are grateful to God Almighty for such a fascinating display of His creation.

28

A Point of View

Investment in equity is the most logical investment for growth. Only if one could time the entry and exit…

Am I animate, inanimate, just a figure, a line on the graph, a mere number, or an average, weighted or floating? I have a personality of my own, but hardly have time to stop by and deliberate. I am ever dynamic, buoyant and changing constantly. I have no privacy to my dismay, and am in full public gaze all the time. My every move is splashed boldly all over and I am under constant scrutiny of millions. Some adore me like a woman they wish to woo. Admire my every step. Some think they understand me. They do not hesitate to stake their fortunes on my trends predicted by experts, who are busy analysing my moods and prophesying my likely behaviour. They run for cover when I do not respond to their predictions. Promptly, the next set of wise men surface and continue the same game, unabashedly repackaging the same old wine in new bottles, knowing fully well that I have hardly any control on my own behaviour. With the melt down lasting too long, they have become wise, and now render confusing and non-committal treatises; the theme being wait and watch, or offer long-term solutions. How long is the long, they leave it to one's imagination. There are myriad forces driving me in multiple directions. Little do they realize that even an innocuous trigger initiated in a remote corner of the globe may set off a massive wave whose ripples may well become the cause for my sharp upswing or downturn. All these thoughts leave me confused. They call me Sensex in India; I could as well be Dow Jones in the USA, FTSE in the UK and the like across the globe. I am considered to be the barometer of Indian capital market; an indicator of the economic state of this huge emerging market. So what exactly am I, and why am I?

I am nothing but a jugglery of jargons and figures coined by those who control me, in keeping with globally-accepted norms for brethren of my kind the world over. By international standards, I am relatively young. Conceived in 1986, with the base year of 1978-79 and the base value of 100, I track 30 stocks representing large, well-established and financially sound companies across the key sectors.[1] These companies are under constant review for their performance to continue to merit tracking by me. Initially, I was calculated on the 'market capitalization method'. My index value was arrived at by calculating the average of the total market capitalization by the total number of shares issued. To this was applied a weightage

---

1. BSE India, www.bseindia.com.

factor for total capitalization value and for the total turnover which was a measure of liquidity. Subsequently, I was switched to a more realistic model of 'free float weighted'. A factor of free float was applied to the weighted average. Free float implied taking into account only the tradable shares. This excluded the 'controlled or strategic holdings', e.g., government holdings, holdings of the promoters, Foreign Direct Investment (FDI) route holdings, locked-in stocks and so on, which de facto were not available for trading. This made me more broad based and reduced concentration of top few companies in the index.

Till the FDI was allowed in, or shall I say encouraged in, Indian capital market was fairly insulated from global buoyancy. But not any more. A sneeze by the Dow Jones Industrial Average, or S&P 500, my elder brothers in the USA, or FTSE 100 of the UK, or Nikkei 225 of Japan, Hang Seng of Shanghai and even to some extent the European indices like CAC 40 of France, and DAX of Germany cause tickles and make me waver immediately or in a staggered time frame. Therefore, I have become more predictable in short-term time frame. The day traders and derivative players thrive making hay of my peaks and troughs. The Foreign Institutional Investors (FIIs) are ever on the prowl. On the slightest margins, they shoot and scoot, exploiting the leverages leaving the small investors high and dry who are unable to time the exit. Exuberance to attract FDI by liberalizing controls is a double-edged weapon. Though it makes the market attractive and global, it becomes vulnerable to global defaults as well. In spite of a hawk's eye and prompt intervention by the regulatory, (RBI and SEBI in my case), the market players innovatively find ways to skirt around and outwit the system. Notwithstanding all this, I continue my unending journey, trying my best to meet the aspirations of those who have reposed their faith in my values. So why am I and in what way do I contribute to the Indian economy?

My importance stems from the fact that I provide a credible guide to the investors on profitability of the stocks of the companies that I track. Although I track only 30 companies, these cover nearly 50 per cent of the total market capitalization. I am, therefore, a reflection of health of the economy. Performance and forecasts of growth by constituent companies, political scenario, economic policies, elections, import/export policies, strength of own currency, major international events, monsoons, natural calamities, etc., all of these factors combined have a direct bearing on my rise and fall. If the investors assess my rise to be genuine, they buy shares, otherwise they sell. With every such turbulence, stock prices change, and as a result the total market capitalization value rises or falls. In other words, I am instrumental in creation or flight of wealth in the market. No wonder, I am the direct measure for investment by passive asset management, that is, mutual funds.

I have a sibling in Nifty, which tracks 50 companies, and is much more versatile with size-based sectoral and derivative-based variants. Yet, more like BSE 100, 200 and 500 represent even a broader segment of the market as they track still larger number of companies. Nonetheless, I have continued to provide a stable parameter of our economy ever since I was launched in 1986. It took me 18 years to rise to value of 6000 by January 2004. Thereafter, the gateways for FDI route became much more attractive for the FIIs. They invested heavily in our market and I rose to 14000 in just three years by January 2007. Next one year was phenomenal; this saw my meteoric rise to dizzy heights of 20000. It is at this time that serpentine effect of the sub prime lending rates and loan defaults in Europe and the USA came to light and the FIIs sensed their vulnerability faster than our domestic investors. They liquidated fast causing my major bust. In spite of heavy props by the Reserve Bank of India and even higher by the Federal Banks and respective governments the world over—in the form of bailing out banks, injecting liquidity by cutting down the interest rates, or cash reserve ratios—I was unable to recover. In between, greed of others like Maddoff and Satyams nailed me down further. And there I was tottering at 9000 in less than a year, with the rock bottom still not in sight. But all was not lost. Indian market showed more resilience. The rot was stemmed. It soon started tracing the path of recovery. I started looking up again and at a much faster pace than the global indices. Therefore my tryst with the investors continues. I reflect on the romantic journey with the investors, and of my pangs and their pleasure and pain.

I recall the era of laid-back pace of changes in my value. It would keep the non-speculative investors busy studying company profiles, and then invest in blue chips; thereafter, sit back for long-term appreciation and dividends in due course. This invariably would happen. Logically too, it should have had; after all, blue chips were big companies, huge infrastructure, great track record, planned growth, adequate reserves, good financial parameters, management ethics, etc. It was a win-win situation for a patient and deliberate investor. Immune to the travails of the global markets, a shift of more than 100 in my value would be termed 'volatile'. Therefore, one had adequate warnings to book profits or to cut losses, which would also not be beyond the comfort zone. Investors would dream about my rise with a romantic flare, watching and predicting my curves with accuracy even to time for intra-day movements. It was thus a playful and safe activity to indulge in, if nothing else then just for fun and experience. Online trading ushered in a totally new ethos and pattern of trading. All of a sudden, many links were just removed by a single stroke. It gave rise to yet another breed of investors, young, confident, tech savvy, and many full timers. Impulsive trading was a complimentary accompaniment to this era. Transformation from the era of pleasure to pain was in the offing.

With the fundamental infrastructure in place and massive knowledge base and young workforce at hand, corporate world of India sensed the opportunity and rose to the occasion. They invested heavily to meet the global challenges of quality and quantity. Sooner than later, industrial growth of India took off at an unbelievably scorching pace. This made Indian stock market the preferred destination for the FIIs. I started rising steadily, and so did the wealth of my investors. It was a pleasure to see the smile on their faces. Soon the events started overtaking me. Rising to the peak, I was as if riding the aggressive bull, unable to get off or control the pace. Some wise investors booked their profits, but most remained naïve, waiting for the slow down to time their exit. And then came the deluge, thanks to the sub-prime lending rates and loan defaults. Value of property and infrastructure crashed overnight to staggering lows. To my dismay, wealth of many of my investors was wiped out. I stood watching as a bystander unable to help. Rehabilitation measures were in full swing, yet the capital continued to disappear. It was some time before I could regain the confidence of the investors. The word 'equity' had become a taboo. The state, 'the day after' was that many players had been wiped out, many had to curtail their levels drastically, there were massive layoffs, pay cuts and foreclosures of property loans. All reeling under the effect of the recession. Yet many hung on in hope. They learnt fast, cut their costs to the bone and remodelled their businesses. Many such players succeeded phenomenally in spite of the recession.

In reflection, I endorse the traditional thought process, 'old times were the best times'. Was such liberalization worth it? We did gain a few hundred billion dollars as an investment, but most of it disappeared without notice. In any case, it was never meant to be locked in. Everyone is now becoming wiser after the event. Keynesian model of capitalism, of greater control by the state for post-great depression of the 30s is in, but rather late. Why can't we consolidate and grow, and control our own pace? Only if one could understand the subtle difference between growth and greed. Have we learnt our lesson? I would rather see the investor in the good old romantic mood celebrating if I rose by 100 points; at least, he smiled, and had a sustained smile. The tears too, if there, be in a trickle and not a flood.

29

My Unfulfilled Aspirations

Life is a zero sum game. You win some; You lose some…

It was a beautiful summer day. Breeze was whistling past. Tall Ashokas were swaying in reverence. The chime was chiming, producing a lulling note. Clouds were not so dark, but there was mild drizzle. Silver lining of the clouds was resplendent. The sun also was struggling to show up. Soothing music was emanating in the distance. The hills far away, very scenic were visibly enjoying the heavy rain. We were sitting in the balcony absorbing the rich ambience. Sipping tea. It was heavenly. The family discussions took a turn when a question was thrown at me. Were there any aspirations which remained unmet and I still yearned for?

After a long innings and a fairly successful career, I was leading an active life. I was pursuing my passions, living the way I wanted to. In the normal course, response to this ought to have been immediate. Automatic or even reflexive. But I drew a blank. This sudden query took me off guard. It took me some time to gather my wits. Collecting my thoughts, I dug deep in my subconscious mind. Were their really any aspirations that I had or set for myself in life and was still missing them? No answer came to my mind. I did recall a number of failures and setbacks. But the rationale of my mind discarded them. None of these seemed to qualify for the honour. These events did not leave much impression on me or my life. The effect, if at all, was momentary in nature in the continuum of my life. On the flip side, there were many successes too. These did give me a thrill, but soon I got used to them and moved ahead. I realized that these were only relative, as yet higher levels of successes had been achieved by many. If one had brooded, this could have given rise to a feeling of despondency for having missed the higher level of success. It would have been comic. A success becoming a source of misery! Fortunately, all this did not even cross my mind.

It appeared that I was content with what I got and did not miss what I did not. Would that mean that I did not have any aspirations? If so, what could have been my motivation? That surely was not the case. How could I have been so dynamic sans any inspiration or motivation? My reluctance for a prompt response and visible dilemma raised the curiosity of everyone present. My life had been so smooth and appeared too good to be true. But there must be some chinks in my armour, or some skeletons in the cupboard. Something still must be eluding me. Everyone wanted to pry. Much that I would have loved to, I could not conjure an honest reply to this simple probe into my life. I decided to parry and seek an adjournment, deferring the discussion to another session. The best course I thought was to sleep over the issue and delve into this with a fresh mind.

To my surprise, with time, the fog started clearing and my response and the rationale started demystifying. I realized that journey of life was like travelling on a long distance train. Successes and failures were like passengers who accompanied you en route, fading away from the memory as speedily as they emerged. Very few continued to accompany till the end. In short, impact of such successes and failures diminished rapidly with time. Once the immediate reaction had sunk in, these tended to merge into each other, leaving one wondering whether it was really a success or a failure. Reason: each of these had positive and negative connotations in varying time domains, viz., in the immediate future or in the long run. But the journey of life continued unruffled.

It was a revelation that I had no aspirations or interchangeably set any long-term goal in my life. It never occurred to me. And what could these be? To be a millionaire? Or to reach the top of the hierarchy? Too far fetched. Too distant. How could one control the external environment and the intangible factors, that too in such a long time span? It had to be one step at a time. Otherwise, one would be tense all the time and perhaps forget to live. Yes, if one had a macro vision or ability to crystal gaze into the future, one could work towards that. It is often said that you can shape your future. But how far and how specifically, still remains a question. I did have some ideas, but these were too ethereal and perhaps virtual in nature. These were more towards my intrinsic growth; ethics, values, attitude, courage of conviction, and ability to learn and excel in whatever one did. All these gave an immeasurable strength to me from within.

I did set short-term goals for myself in my professional life. However, success or failure of these only had a notional impact. In profession, the credit for the successes has a habit of gravitating upwards in the hierarchy. The same holds true for failures, but in the opposite direction. These really did not matter in the long journey of life. All that mattered was the perceptions of the hierarchy. In spite of having performed to the best of one's ability, recognition for the actions or glossing over the omissions lay in the eyes of those in control. After all, there is a very thin red line between valour and cowardice. It is the perception. This is where destiny steps in.

I believe good luck is not a bonanza falling in your lap like a lottery, but merely in getting your due. I know many brilliant colleagues falling by the wayside and many a mediocre reaching dizzying heights. This is not really a cause for anguish or thrill as long as one is clear that an honest effort has been put in. Such a rise or otherwise deserves the importance in life only if you choose to patronize this emotion psychologically. Viewed dispassionately, nothing really has changed as far as the person himself is concerned. He is still the same in flesh and blood. Crux of the matter is what you think of yourself. Do you regret any of your genuine actions? Did you have the courage to shoulder responsibility for your actions, or did you unhesitatingly share or pass down the credit as due and not usurped it yourself? Do you enjoy the respect of your family and colleagues? If the answers to all these is in the affirmative, then you are still a winner. That much for short-term goals, albeit aspirations. After all, life is a package. It finally balances out. It is a zero sum game; you win some, you lose some.

The sum total of above deliberations reinforced my belief to remain natural without putting up a façade and be indifferent to the results of my actions, assuming the actions to be sincere, honest and to the best of my ability. Simply put, one learns and performs to excel. This lends dignity to the effort. The rest should follow. If, for some reason, it does not, then it ought not to be a matter of anguish or deterrence for future actions. One has to draw upon one's inner strength for courage and confidence. Once one learns to disassociate from the results, one becomes so involved with his actions that nothing else really matters. The mind becomes free; free to soar across the boundaries and be creative. One is then in a constant state of bliss. This becomes one's eternal source of inspiration.

Coincidentally, this is synonymous to the theory of karma that Lord Krishna propounded to the legendary warrior Arjuna, hero of the famous epic *Mahabharata*. The warrior was reluctant to take up arms against his own kith and kin, in spite of their misdoings. On the eve of the battle, the Lord decided to explain to Arjuna the meaning of karma and responsibility of a person to act and not retract. He said that one ought to act and yet remain detached from the results, be there a credit or discredit in this. This is the course that a *karma yogi*, the doer, should follow. He should act and not hold back. This differentiates him from those following the middle path, deciding to sit on the fence, and turn the way the wind blows. It is possible some such person may rise in life but with what conviction? He may also attempt to manipulate the future. But fooling whom and for how long? This is where the intangibles but vital factors of ethics, values, contentment, internal peace, and satisfaction come to the fore. Perhaps, these are the real motivating factors for one's behaviour and actions. It would now be appropriate to correlate and apply the above rationale realistically to myself in relation to the issue under deliberation.

In all humility, I don't prophesize to be a *karma yogi* or any high flying doer. Looking deep in my past, I realize that I have been a simple and straight forward person who did have ambitions but was not ambitious. I was neither charismatic nor did I pose to be one. I started my career with a serious handicap. I lacked basic proficiency in many fields. But what I did have was an urge to learn and put in an honest effort. My ambitions were limited to the immediate or near future, and were pitched at the level of my capability. There were very little materialistic ambitions in me. I had inherited the treasure of values. My main achievement may have been in holding on to these and strengthening them further.

I distinctly recall many occasions in having taken crucial decisions with conviction, knowing fully well that these may be contrary to the party line. I was prepared for the consequences. After all, when lives or careers of so many were at stake on my judgment or decisions, how could I discriminate, or be untruthful to myself or my organization? I was fortunate; I came out as winner most of the times. I was astonished to learn that I was considered a role model by many of my junior colleagues. I am not sure what they had actually observed, but I did realize that people are looking for transparency of mind, openness and no double standards. Rest of the achievements are only like cherry on the cake. These have been and still are my motivating factors and my long-term aspirations I suppose. And these seemingly have been met to a large extent.

But I am no saint; I do have my moments of thrill. I love life and live from day-to-day. How I love to remain fit, spend time on it and yet not like to waste time. How I am excited like a child looking forward to a good game of squash. How I love to putt all the four-footers and get my share of pars in a round of golf. What thrill I get if a pretty girl says 'hi' and does not add 'uncle'. How I wish to have a flat stomach. What excitement I get when I start reading a new book. How I love to be busy creatively, be it in reading or writing. How I love to be in the open in rain. How I love to watch the tall trees sway on a windy day. How I love to see my Labrador curl up and favour me with her affections. The list goes on. All these appear to be small, but these have a habit of playing hide and seek with me. I am continuing to work in that direction and derive my contentment from these small things. Fortified with the above revelations about myself, I felt I had the answers, and was ready for the deferred session of family discussions.